Caring for
DOGS

Caring for
DOGS

LLYFRAU 'R YNYS
ISLAND BOOKS
PRODUCED FOR S.WEBB & SON
Menai Bridge

This 2000 edition is published by
S. WEBB & SON Distributors LTD.
Telford Place
Pentraeth Road
Menai Bridge
Isle of Anglesey
LL59 5RW

Printed in Italy

ISBN 1 85361 470 X

Picture Acknowledgements

All photographs supplied through the **RSPCA Photolibrary** with the exception of those on pages 17 below left, 36 all, (apart from below right which is ©Angela Hampton) which are © **Regency House Publishing Limited**..
The following are ©RSPCA Photolibrary and the following photographers: Cover pages RSPCA, title pages Geoff du Feu: this page Andrew Forsyth: opposite Colin Seddon: page 10 Angela Hampton, page 11 top Klaus-Peter Wolf: page 11 below left Colin Seddon, below centre and right E.A. Janes: page 12 both Gunther Kopp: page 13 above Angela Hampton, below E.A. Janes: pages 14 and 15 all Angela Hampton: page 16 above Geoff du Feu, below Angela Hampton: page 17 above left Angela Hampton, above right Mark Hamblin, below right Colin Seddon: page 18 left Angela Hampton, right above and below E.A. Janes: page 19 Mark Hamblin: page 20 above E.A. Janes, below Angela Hampton: page 21 Mark Hamblin: page 22 above left Colin Seddon, above right Maria Imperi, below Cheryl Ertelt: page 23 Colin Seddon: Page 24 both E.A. Janes: page 25 above left Nigel Rolstone, below left Angela Hampton, right Alan Robinson: page 26 above E.A. Janes, below Angela Hampton: page 27 Angela Hampton: page 28 above left Steve Cobb, above left Angela Hampton, below Andrew Forsyth: page 29 left E.A. Janes, right top left Colin Seddon, top right and bottom left E.A. Janes, bottom right Del Photographic, below right top Andrew Forsyth, bottom Colin Seddon: page 30 both Angela Hampton: page 31 above E.A. Janes, below Ken McKay: page 32 above E.A. Janes, below Angela Hampton: page 33 above left Mark Hamblin, above right and below Angela Hampton: page 34 above Mark Hamblin, below Angela Hampton: page 35 both Angela Hampton: page 37 above left Angela Hampton, above right Tim Sambrook, below Ken McKay: page 38 Colin Seddon: page 39 above J.B. Blossom, below Mark Hamblin: page 40 Colin Seddon: page 41 left Andrew Forsyth, right above and below Angela Hampton: page 42 above Dave Bevan, below J.B. Blossom: page 43 E.A. Janes: page 44 above Robert Jones, below all Andrew Forsyth: page 45 above Andrew Linscott, below Cheryl Ertelt: page 46 both Angela Hampton: page 47 E.A. Janes: page 48 Angela Hampton: page 49 Duncan I. McEwan: page 50 above J.B. Blossom, below Geoff du Feu: page 51 above Angela Hampton, below left J.B. Blossom, below right Andrew Forsyth: page 52 left S. Thompson, right above and below Angela Hampton: page 53 Des Cartwright: page 54 above Tim Sambrook, below Mark Hamblin: page 55 left and above right Angela Hampton, below E.A. Janes: pages 56 and 57 all Angela Hampton: page 58 above Angela Hampton, below left Tim Sambrook, below right Colin Seddon: page 59 both Angela Hampton: page 60 both Angela Hampton: page 61 above Angela Hampton, below Des Cartwright: page 62 above both Angela Hampton, below E.A. Janes: page 63 below Angela Hampton: pages 64 and 65 all Angela Hampton: page 66 both Angela Hampton: page 67 above Colin Seddon, below left Des Cartwright, below right Angela Hampton: page 68 above E.A. Janes, below Angela Hampton: page 69 above Des Cartwright, below Colin Seddon: page 70 above June Hassall, below E.A. Janes: page 71 above Angela Hampton, below Des Cartwright: page 73 above Angela Hampton, below Geoff du Feu: page 74 Steve Cobb: pages 75–75 Angela Hampton.
The publisher would like to thank the Royal Society for the Prevention of Cruelty to Animals for supplying these wonderful pictures.

Contents

Introduction

Above right: The mixed-bred dog makes an ideal companion. He is bright, affectionate and largely free from the hereditary defects common in pedigree dogs.

Below left: This Tibetan Mastiff puppy will grow into a large handsome dog. He requires plenty of exercise and will cost a good deal to keep but with firm but kind training will become a rewarding member of the family.

Below centre: The Fox Terrier is extremely alert but has a distinct tendency to be wilful. Training should begin as early as possible.

Below right: These two Irish Setters are elegance and grace personified, but with their long feathered chestnut coats will require daily grooming. They are lively and active dogs and require a good deal of regular exercise.

Opposite: This Labrador is in his element when he is the centre of his family's attention. Dogs are of benefit to children, teaching them respect and kindness towards all animals. However, when both dog and child are young, a close eye should be kept on both.

Watch-dog, working-dog, show-dog, family pet – whatever your aims and requirements it is ultimately down to you, the owner, to raise your dog to be respectful, obedient and as healthy as possible. A dog raised in a sympathetic environment, which has at all times been handled kindly but firmly, is a pleasure to own and his intelligence, grace and unique character will endear him to all. As a species, the dog's fidelity and devotion is legendary. Make sure you reward his trust by always treating him with diplomacy and respect.

It is interesting to note that there are remarkable social similarities between man and *canis familiaris*; we are both naturally gregarious and enjoy living and co-operating with others of our species. In the wild, the dog is a pack animal and it is this trait which explains how man and dog can live and work well together, man of course coming to be regarded by his dog as his pack leader. This must be reinforced by careful training, otherwise the dog will come to think that he has the upper hand and quickly degenerate into a pest and a nuisance.

The aim is to offer sensible, practical advice that is easy for existing owners to understand as well as for those contemplating dog ownership for the first time. Choice of breed, advice on acquiring a dog, raising puppies, health and fitness, equipment, exercise and training and much more are all thoroughly explored, as well as the commonest behavioural problems which may occur and how to correct them. Keep this handbook by you for easy reference to dip into when required.

Never forget that the decision to acquire a dog is a serious matter and should not be entered into lightly. Remember that he will rely on you for most of his needs and may live and be dependent on you for up to 18 years. However, once gained, a dog's love and trust in you is a joyful experience which cannot fail but enrich both your lives.

Chapter One
A Wolf in the House

From the Great Dane to the smallest of toy breeds, all dogs are direct descendants of the wolf and many of the wolf's characteristics still survive in today's domestic breeds. Once the wolf ran wild over many parts of the world, its keen intelligence and strong pack instinct making it a formidable hunter where it lived a co-operative life and hunted as a group. Unfortunately, the wild wolf population has greatly declined, though some manage to survive in Canada, parts of Asia and in limited numbers in Europe.

Man's association with the wolf began after the last ice age when the wolf was an extremely successful animal, trailing large groups of hoofed animals north across the ever-receding ice. Man, the only other species to move north at this time also hunted these beasts. So, in a gradual process, some wolves began to socialize with man. The wolf cubs were very appealing, and men took them into their homes, raising them with their own families or tribe (pack). The young wolves were not slow in recognizing the similarity of the family to their own pack structure and quickly became accustomed to living with man who gradually assumed the role of overall pack leader. So over the course of years, some wolves moved from the forests and mountains to sleep by warm fires and receive good meals in return for work done. Man soon realized that the wolf's natural hunting instincts could be conveniently harnessed and this became an important part of their evolution into companion and working animals. Gradually, through selective breeding, the wolf/dog's appearance changed to suit man's requirements, making the dog a largely man-made invention while retaining elements of a wolf's personality.

By quietly observing our own dogs, one gets an interesting insight into the way their lupine forebears lived: wolves like to gather in large packs and a group of dogs left to run free will follow the same rituals of hunting, resting, feeding and sleeping together for warmth and protection. The strongest animal, usually a male, will dominate, growling and baring its teeth in a display of its dominance over the pack. The ancient wolf-pack instinct is immediately apparent in the way subservient animals roll over or cower, this behaviour being nowadays largely ritualistic and instinctive.

Opposite above: Man's association with the wolf can be traced back to the end of the ice age. They had similar characteristics in that they formed family/pack groups and needed to co-operate when hunting, bringing them into closer proximity as they travelled north in the wake of the receding ice.

Opposite below: Man could hardly fail to be enchanted by the wolf cub, the ancestor of the domestic dog, taking it into his own home and raising it as a hunting companion and member of his own family.

Above right: The modern dog still retains many of the traits of its wild ancestor. When running free with other dogs, he quickly becomes aware of his position in the pack, displaying many of the characteristics of wolves in the wild and even submitting to a similar 'pecking' order. It is this pack instinct which makes your dog co-operate with you as a member of your human 'pack' or family.

Right: The hunting instinct is as alive and well in the dog as it is in the wolf and man has managed to harness the dog's innate talents to his own ends. This sheepdog is strongly driven by his own ancient instincts as he herds sheep, and it is only the control of the pack leader, the shepherd, which restrains him from catching a sheep and killing it for food.

But in a wild wolf pack, it was important that the pecking order be maintained for the stability of the group, even though it could result in a fight to the death.

In the process of its domestication and transition from wolf to domestic animal, the dog has developed a unique bond with us, sharing our homes, working alongside us, and offering us its faithful and unswerving loyalty. The dog was among the first of the animals to live as members of our households, appearing to enjoy our company while at the same time being useful hunters and fierce protectors. The dog had a remarkable capacity to cope with change and was soon able to settle happily into this new environment and work for us in return for a comfortable home where he became devoted to his master, offering such a remarkable degree of faithfulness that his name has become synonymous with the word. The dog's role in our lives has changed very little since those early times, except that these days he has come to be regarded more as a pet than a working companion, a creature we have grown to love and who adds an indefinable richness to our lives.

The Useful Dog

As already mentioned, a dog's behaviour is directly linked to its ancient wolf ancestry and its place in the pack, and many of these natural traits have been put to good use in his long association with man. Dogs are gregarious and co-operative in relation to others of their species; if you watch dogs together, they will eat, drink, play and sleep at the same time, and this will largely be echoed in their relationship with you. You will find, therefore, that when you are sitting down quietly watching TV, or even asleep, your dog will be right there beside you and if you get up, he will get up. This type of communal behaviour has naturally developed into an act of companionship with man in which the dog is unique, no other animal having developed this trait to such an extent apart from, perhaps, the cat.

It is for this reason that dogs are suited to teamwork. When huskies are put to the task of pulling a sled, or are members of a pack of hunting dogs, they are re-enacting the wolf-pack behaviour of the wild, the only difference this time being that the ultimate pack leader is man.

Other forms of behaviour stem from territorial marking. In the wild, the wolf's territory is very strictly delineated. The dog's sense of smell is extremely acute, and he is aware of our approach even before he sees us. Dogs also like to mark their territory using their saliva, urine and faeces. Male dogs cock their legs up high so that the odour is easy to detect, and some dogs kick up the ground as well as a visual warning to other dogs. This trait is utilized by hunters, as is the dog's keen hearing which is superior to ours. He is swiftly able to detect a scuttling rat or an animal deep underground; he can sniff out objects, making him useful in detecting and bringing to our attention the presence of illegal drugs and explosives. Dogs have a much wider range of

vision than us, allowing them to perceive hazards and objects before we do. Their vision, however, is biased towards the red end of the spectrum.

A sense of territory is very strong in dogs, which is a characteristic we exploit when we train them as guard dogs. However, this form of aggression must be strictly curbed as it can be dangerous when allowed to get out of control.

The wolf is a competent hunter and catches its prey through a combination of stalking, constructive herding and running, all these things being present in the dog, which is why they cannot resist chasing after moving objects. This natural instinct can be put to good use and dogs have been selectively bred to turn this to our advantage in the sheepdog, for example, which combines herding instincts with sparkling intelligence and total obedience to the shepherd, who issues instructions through specific whistles and gestures.

Above: The dog has developed a remarkable rapport with man, regarding us as his leader and trusting us completely. Even when required to do something as unnatural as sailing, the dog is content to be with his master.

Below: These dogs are happy to share food and will also play and sleep together, as would wolves. This behaviour is echoed in his contact with man in that he will rest when you are sitting and get up when you do.

Chapter Two
Choosing a Dog

Before deciding that you would like to be a dog owner, you must ask yourself and your family some important questions. A dog can live for a long time, and he will require daily exercise and companionship as well as discipline and love. Unlike cats, which come and go as they please, dogs cannot be left alone for long periods of time and will fret if neglected.

However, once selected, your dog will become an important member of the family. Children will welcome him as a playmate, and in the process of growing up together they will become devoted friends. Owning a dog, along with other pets, teaches children from an early age to take responsibility for another living creature and teaches them to show respect and gentleness to animals smaller than themselves.

Owning a cat or a dog is said to produce a calming effect and is thought to even be useful in lowering high blood pressure. These days, groups of owners can be seen taking their own dogs around hospitals where the sick and elderly can also enjoy them, and this has proved a useful therapy and aid to recovery. Likewise a smaller,

Above: Dogs make wonderful pets: they offer comfort and companionship to those who are sick or elderly as well as offering their protection and even helping people to cope with disabilities such as deafness or blindness.

Dogs have recently been introduced to hospitals and hospices where it has been demonstrated that their presence can help lessen stress and reduce blood pressure, as well as speeding up the recovery process and offering comfort and consolation.

Left: Children love dogs and dogs love children and it is not unknown for a dog to save a child's life. Children must be taught from an early age to have respect for all animals and treat them with kindness and diplomacy.

sedate dog is the perfect pet for an elderly person, especially for those living alone, as they provide a high degree of companionship and protection. There have been many instances of dogs saving their owners' lives, rescuing people from drowning, and even warning of imminent danger. Again, their natural attributes have been turned to our own benefit. The Saint Bernard with its large paws and thick coat can easily plough through thick snow to help with a mountain rescue, and the Newfoundland with its webbed feet and natural love of swimming has been used to rescue the drowning. In addition, dogs are trained to be the eyes and ears of the blind and deaf, to protect our homes, and to patrol busy harbours and airports, searching out explosives and illegal substances.

Choose your dog according to your own and your family's needs; for example, if you enjoy long walks it would be sensible to select a dog with good stamina. There are many breeds which require a good deal of exercise, and many cross-breeds make ideal walking companions. If you prefer to just amble around, or cannot walk very far, choose a more sedentary breed.

If you have young children in the house, don't choose an aggressive breed. You may be attracted to a Rottweiler as it is indeed a handsome dog, but the breed requires strict and correct handling. A dog of this type could unwittingly harm a child, whereas many breeds will actually protect and look out for a child's welfare.

Do I Have Time for a Dog?

As mentioned before, dogs should not be left alone for long periods of time as they are extremely sociable animals and thrive in company. Of course if somebody is at home all day this is the ideal situation, and some have been known to take their dogs to work with them. If you

Above: Walking the dog is fun for all the family as well as being healthy and bracing for you all. Despite its athletic build, the Greyhound needs only moderate exercise.

Left: Include your dog in as many family activities as possible. He would rather be out and about with you than left at home to pine on his own.

Opposite
Above left: This little cross-breed has been especially trained to be the ears of her deaf owner.

Above right: The West Highland White Terrier has great charm as well as vitality and intelligence. It requires regular gentle exercise, and makes an ideal pet for the moderately energetic.

Below left: This charming cross-bred terrier-type is the perfect companion. He is strong and healthy with an alert expression, and possesses great stamina. He is ideal as a family pet but requires a good deal of exercise.

Below right: The Jack Russell Terrier has grown in popularity. He is brave, a great watchdog for his size, and a good ratter. Despite his small size he requires a fair amount of exercise, and will greatly enjoy a good game of tug. Can be aggressive with other dogs.

cannot be with your dog all day, make sure that a friend can come in and visit him a couple of times a day. Perhaps you could take him for a walk in your lunch break; a brisk walk will quickly tire him so that he will be much more relaxed and not too unhappy to be left alone.

Two dogs provide good company for one another, but only if they have plenty of space. However, this is no excuse for leaving them alone for long periods of time. It is also possible that when more than one dog is left alone there may be a reversion to pack behaviour and they may forget that their human owner has now assumed the role as leader. Don't be tempted to leave a dog in a car or tied up outside: in both cases this is extremely cruel and could even be fatal.

Dogs are athletic creatures, happiest when at their peak of fitness. Ideally, two good walks a day are enough to keep them healthy and happy. Dogs do not necessarily need to run free, but if you live in an area with large open spaces this is obviously preferable. Take a rubber ball with you and you can both have fun teaching him to retrieve it. If you must keep your dog on a leash because you live in a busy urban area, you will have to walk further, but regard this as a bonus in that you yourself are getting fit along with him.

Before you choose a dog, look carefully at your particular environment. If you live in a small flat in town, get a small dog which requires less space or even consider an older, more sedate animal. There are plenty of beautiful older dogs desperately in need of a loving home. If you live in a larger house with a yard or garden and plenty of space, you may prefer a larger or more active dog; but remember, they will require a great deal of exercise.

If you live a busy life, don't buy a long-haired dog which requires meticulous grooming; a shorter-haired variety requires only a quick brush a couple of times a week, whereas one with longer hair will require intensive daily grooming.

Finally, before introducing a dog into your household, make sure that the other members agree; dogs thrive on love and attention and will quickly sense when a person dislikes them and may resort to inappropriate behaviour. Don't buy a dog if there is an asthma sufferer or a person allergic to animal hair. If you have a very young baby or are pregnant, it is wiser to wait until the child is older before introducing a new dog as they carry diseases harmful to the young and unborn and may well harbour jealous feelings towards a new-born baby. Obviously an older, established dog will require careful monitoring in the presence of children and extra attention to hygiene should be observed.

Above: Known as 'Lassie' dogs from the popular film and TV series, the Rough Collie is a popular choice as it is affectionate and enjoys family life. They require a moderate amount of exercise as well as daily grooming.

Left: The Labrador Retriever is well known for its kind and even temperament. It is easy to train and very good with children, a fact which is well demonstrated here.

Opposite: These adorable Border Collie puppies are not for the faint-hearted for, as adults, they require vigorous exercise. But they are extremely intelligent and excellent subjects for obedience training.

Below: The German Shepherd can be trained to do many different jobs. They require kind but firm handling by an experienced adult. They have rather a reserved nature, but once their trust is earned will be unquestionably loyal. They can suffer from a variety of genetic disorders, so it is advisable to buy only from a reputable breeder.

Choosing the Right Dog for You

Once you are satisfied that you can fullfil all the requirements of dog ownership and are confident that you can provide a loving and caring home, you are ready to begin your search for an animal you can live with.

There are a vast array of breeds from which to choose, from the tiny Chihuahua to the Great Dane. All have their unique character traits and by careful selection you should be able to find a dog which fits well with your lifestyle. For example: if you are the type of person who lives in the country and regularly enjoys taking long bracing walks you may consider one of the more active working breeds, such as a Springer Spaniel or a Border Collie. These dogs are bred to work out-of-doors in fields and woods all day; they thrive on exercise and if deprived of it may develop undesirable behavioural problems. Don't be fooled by size: many of the smaller breeds also require a surprising amount of vigorous exercise.

For those who prefer a short stroll twice a day, consider one of the larger breeds, such as the St. Bernard and Newfoundland which, though large, are dogs which prefer a more sedentary life, or a little toy breed which you will find easy to tire. Think long and hard before buying a long-haired breed; for example, Afghan Hounds and Old English Sheepdogs have beautiful luxurious coats, but require daily intensive grooming to avoid

knots and mats from forming, which are not only extremely unattractive but painful to remove. If you lead a busy life and are short of time, choose a low-maintenance short-haired breed such as a Pointer or Doberman or a rough-coated animal such as a Jack Russell or Border Terrier. These require only a quick brush once or twice a week.

It is vital to thoroughly examine your environment as some dogs are really happiest outdoors. Huskies, for example, have very thick coats designed to cope with extremely harsh temperatures, so don't buy one if you live in a warm, centrally-heated apartment. Others, such as the thin-coated Whippet, Greyhound and some of the toy breeds, will actually relish the luxury of your home.

Temperament is another highly important factor. If you are introducing a dog into a family of small children and other animals, it is wise to choose a breed known for its kind temperament such as a Labrador or even an animal of mixed breeding. It is also preferable to introduce a puppy to this type of household, as young children are less likely to be seriously bitten and other animals will accept him as he is still too little to pose a threat.

All dogs require a certain standard of training, most of which can be done in the home. But some of the larger, more aggressive breeds will require professional training so, before acquiring one of these, make sure that you are prepared and have the time to attend dog-training classes.

Many people have a firm notion of the kind of dog they want, being automatically drawn to the pedigree variety. When choosing a dog of this type, make sure that you buy from a reputable breeder as pedigree puppies which are sold in pet shops are likely to have come from puppy farms. Not only is this a cruel practice with the mother dog being kept in horrendous conditions, there is also no guarantee that the puppy has not been badly bred when it could develop hereditary diseases such as hip dysplasia, hearing difficulties and eye and skin problems. So however appealing, always follow the rule of never buying a puppy without seeing it with its mother. This way you can be sure that the puppy has been carefully bred in the correct environment.

There are many ways of discovering the type of dog which will appeal to you, the best way being to attend some of the larger dog shows. Here, all the breeds are on display and you will be able to take down names and addresses of the breeders exhibiting there. Another way is by word of mouth, or you could ask your local vet or kennel club, or consult the advertising columns of dog-breeding magazines or local newspapers or, a method which is becoming increasingly more popular, you could look on the internet, as many breeders now have their own web sites.

Breeders are only too aware of the inherited faults likely to appear in pedigree dogs and will do their best to eradicate them from their puppies. Although usually more expensive, it is preferable to buy from a professional breeder as they have their reputations to consider and will be most unlikely to pass on a puppy with serious problems. The amateur who breeds puppies for sale from their own dog as a hobby would not necessarily be as aware of the pitfalls involved in breeding and should also be avoided.

Many people swear by cross- or mixed-breeds. They are invariably hardier, rarely suffering from the congenital diseases to which pedigree dogs are prone. They are usually of good disposition and while it is often difficult to determine the kind of dog such a puppy will grow into, they are more than likely to make excellent pets. Look at the parents to get an idea of your puppy's eventual size. There are many puppies and adult dogs of mixed breeding who desperately require homes, so consider one of these as an important option.

The Advantages of Choosing an Older Dog

There are many thousands of beautiful dogs, both of mixed breeding and, to a lesser degree, pedigree types made homeless for a variety of reasons. These sadly end up in city pounds or dog homes and need desperately to be rehomed. Most homes are run in a professional manner, each dog being cleaned, fed and checked over thoroughly by a vet, where they are also wormed and given a

Above: The little Yorkshire Terrier was originally bred for ratting; however, with its attractive coat and diminutive size it has become a popular pet. Its long silky coat requires daily attention to keep it in pristine condition.

Left: The elegant silver-coated Weimaraner requires firm handling by an experienced adult. However, they are intelligent and have amiable dispositions. Bred as working dogs, they require a great deal of exercise to prevent them from becoming bored.

Opposite: This black Labrador Retriever is a most active dog, with its solid powerful body and handsome looks and thrives on hard work and play. The breed has a history of working hard in roles ranging from sled dog to fisherman's companion. They continue this tradition to this day and are widely used in the police force and as guide dogs for the blind.

Above left: Taking on an older dog has many advantages. Most adult dogs are already house-trained, they have grown out of the destructive puppy stage, and are ready to go outside to play. Many dogs in rehoming centres aren't pedigree animals, but this Spaniel cross is just as handsome as any pure-bred.

Above: The Poodle comes in three different sizes: toy, miniature and standard. It has a long curly coat which keeps on growing and doesn't shed, making it an ideal choice for allergy sufferers.

Left: Never take on a adult Rottweiler, particularly if you don't know its background. Even a puppy should only be handled by an experienced adult. Not really a pet for the home, they make excellent guard dogs.

course of the necessary inoculations. Where possible, a detailed history is made; for example, did the dog once live happily alongside children and other animals; does he require a lot of exercise and has he a history of good health. Where the history is not so well known, tests can be made to determine his likely character and temperament. Once a dog is chosen, one of the staff is likely to come to your home to check its suitability, when you will be given a trial period to make doubly sure that you and your chosen dog are compatible.

Don't choose an older dog on a whim or because you feel sorry for him. Bringing a full-grown dog into your home is a major event and a great upheaval and you will need to ask some important questions before taking him on. For example: is he house-trained, is he well-mannered and of a sound disposition, does he like children and does he respect other animals? Unless you can be totally sure of the answers to all these questions, leave well alone.

However, once you are satisfied that all is as well as can be expected, choosing an older dog has enormous advantages.

He already knows how to behave, he won't grow any bigger, and he will be so grateful to be in a loving home at last that he will surely appreciate and reward your kindness. In return, you will have the joy of seeing him happy and gaining in confidence as he settles into a daily routine. It is not a good idea to take a stray dog in off the streets, or take on the pet of someone you don't know very well; it could well have dangerous behavioural problems and may even carry disease. Always choose from a well run, reputable dog's home.

Below: The attractive Bearded Collie has a friendly and lively disposition. As a working dog, they have great stamina and therefore as a pet require a good deal of exercise. They have a long, luxuriant coat which requires a thorough daily grooming.

The Advantages of Choosing a Puppy

Other than the obvious appeal all young animals possess, there are many advantages in obtaining a puppy. He will grow and develop with your family, becoming accustomed to children and other animals in the household in a completely natural way. He will be bright and alert and a joy to watch; he will relish a game and happily and quickly interact with the entire household. If you choose a puppy of mixed parentage, make sure that you see both mother and father and any grown-up siblings first, then there won't be any unpleasant surprises when your cute little puppy turns into an enormous great hound.

Before bringing your puppy home, carefully follow the following advice. It should be round about 8 weeks old. Make sure that you see the entire litter playing together before making your choice and that puppies and mother are happy, healthy and well-nourished. Closely observe the manner in which they play together and choose one which is behaving happily and normally, one that is not too aggressive but which is not shy or cowering either. Don't pick the runt of the litter: he is likely to have health problems as he grows up. Once selected, pick up the puppy and let him get to know you, making sure that he is comfortable being handled; this is an indication that he has previously been treated kindly. Give him a thorough examination, checking that his body is strong, that his limbs are straight and that he is standing square. Watch him running and playing, making sure that he moves evenly with no sign of lameness. His skin should be clear and pink with no oily patches or flaky skin (the belly is a good place to check for this as it is almost bald at this age). Feel all over

Above: These 7-week-old Whippet puppies will make wonderful pets and are sure to be docile and obedient. However, they are highly-strung and sensitive and can be nervous with strangers.

Left: This Jack Russell mother is with her last remaining puppy which is waiting to go to his new home.

Opposite above: These little Beagles are tired out after a good play. Beagles are good natured and will get on with all the family. Even though they can be wilfull and are difficult to train, their small size makes them manageable.

Opposite below: Puppies and children usually grow up together to become devoted companions. This Boxer will need to be disciplined from an early age, but is easy to train despite his exuberant personality.

the body, checking that there are no lumps or abrasions (this could indicate a flea allergy), and his fur should be clean and glossy, with no signs of moulting. The anus should be clean with no swellings or irritation. Ensure that the ears are clean with no discharge and that there is no unpleasant odour coming from them. The eyes should be clean and bright with no signs of discharge, and the nose cold and wet, also with no discharge. Finally the gums should be a healthy pink colour with no abrasions, the teeth white, and the breath sweet. The general appearance should be one of brightness and alertness and he should be showing a keen interest in his surroundings.

What to Look For in a Healthy Puppy

Ears Should be clean and pink inside, free of any discharge or redness and with no unpleasant odour.

Eyes Should be clear and bright, and the under-lids should be a healthy pink. There should be no redness or watering.

Nose Should be cold and wet when awake, with no discharge or sneezing.

Mouth Breath should be pleasant-smelling, the teeth straight and white, and the gums pink.

Anus Should be free of any swelling or irritation as well as clean and dry.

Skin Should be clean and free from dandruff, blemishes and sore patches.

Coat Should be clean and shiny, with no bald itchy patches. Check for evidence of fleas.

Body Should be symmetrical and well grown. Body movements should be agile and supple.

Limbs There should be no evidence of lameness. The puppy should be able to stand squarely and be active and fluid in his movements.

Chapter Three
Bringing Your Dog Home

Above right: When introducing an older dog into your household you will find that he needs lots of care and attention to make him feel at home. Right from the start, make sure that you establish any no-go areas, such as certain rooms and furniture that he must not lie on.

This little Whippet looks very content on the sofa and her owner is happy for her to sleep there.

Right: Allow your new arrival plenty of time to become adjusted to his new surroundings. This Bearded Collie has finished exploring indoors and is very keen to start looking around outside.

Opposite: This little Boxer puppy is quite content in his comfortable bed, with a hide bone for company. Place the bed in a quiet corner, but not too far away from the bustle of family life so that he feels that he belongs. Just like human babies, puppies need their sleep so, when he decides to settle down, leave him in peace.

The time has arrived to introduce the newcomer to your family home. Remember that this will be a strange experience for you both at first. An older dog needs to be treated with tact, diplomacy and kindness. If he has come from a dog's home he is likely to have had limited space at his disposal, and while the staff try to give as much love as they can, their attention is considerably over-stretched. Consequently, your new friend may either be overwhelmed or thoroughly overexcited. Allow time for him to settle, let him have a good sniff around the house and garden so that he can become accustomed to the new sights and scents with which he will be bombarded. This is also the best time to firmly establish any areas that are forbidden to him; once he has been allowed upstairs or on the sofa you will find it very difficult to stop him in future.

Once all the excitement has subsided, show him his bed. Ideally, you will have managed to keep something from his former home which he recognizes. This will be useful in confirming that this is now his place and offer him a little comfort in a new environment.

The bed itself should be large enough to accommodate him comfortably, made of a sturdy material and filled with comfortable washable bedding. Give him a small portion of food to begin with, as he may be disoriented by the journey, and show him where his water bowl is.

Good preparation is most important. A puppy can be messier than a baby – you can hardly protect him with a diaper. For most of the time it is advisable to restrict him to a place that is not carpeted or covered with expensive flooring material. The kitchen will possibly be chosen as the most frequented family room ensuring that the puppy does not feel excluded or lonely. Allocate a place for his food and water bowls and make him a comfortable bed; puppies feel happier in a warm enclosed space – a box turned onto its side and filled with washable bedding is ideal and can easily be replaced when chewed, or you can buy ready-made enclosed beds. Site the bed in the warmth and away from draughts in a place where he can feel one of the family. While your dog or puppy is sleeping, leave him in peace and remember that puppies can sleep for up to 20 hours a day, requiring ample rest as part of the growing process. Don't let your children disturb him, however eager they are to play.

An enclosed pen is often a good idea. This will limit the area in which a dog can soil and keep him out of trouble when you are unable to keep an eye on him. However, don't use it as a constant excuse to keep him out of the way; puppies need to play and socialize with the family and they also need to be trained to defecate outside; he will never learn if he is kept constantly cooped up. Keep plenty of newspaper and disinfectant to hand and clean up any accidents immediately.

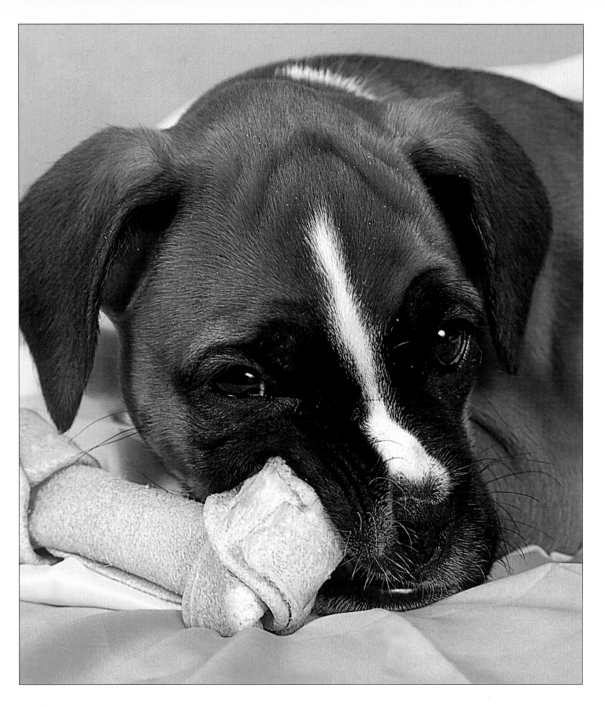

Settling In

The first few days of your dog's arrival are going to seem strange to you both. If you have a puppy you will by now be very familiar with house-training (pages 33–34). A puppy must not be allowed to run around in public places until he has had all his vaccinations when he is about 12–14 weeks old, so he will have to be confined to house and garden. Use this time to get to know one another, introducing him to other members of the family and praising him regularly so that he learns to recognize your voice.

Night-times may prove troublesome, with the puppy whimpering because he fears to be left alone. While he is very young, a clock wrapped in a cloth and placed beside him can fool him into thinking it is his mother's heartbeat, and provide him with a little comfort. He will soon realize that night is a time for settling down to a good long sleep.

Introduce the new arrival to other pets gradually, as they may be rather indignant at losing their prime positions of importance in the household. A good way is to put the puppy in a pen so that the others can sniff him through the bars. Once they have met properly, make a huge fuss of all the animals to minimize the risk of jealousy. Feed separately to avoid quarrels until all are comfortable in each other's company. Once firm friendships are established, the other animals may well be able to offer comfort and companionship to the new arrival and even cats may enjoy cuddling up to a dog for warmth.

Far left: This puppy is relaxing in a heavy and durable, chew-proof plastic basket, filled with comfortable bedding.

Left: This little chap is resting in his beanbag. These are warm and comfortable and come in a variety of colours and sizes. The covers are removable and machine-washable.

Below: Choose the bowl to fit your dog's size and shape. There are even bowls specially designed for dogs with long ears.

Opposite top: A selection of collars and identity tags from which to make your choice.

Opposite left: This Boxer is ready to go out. He has a leather collar and leash and is also wearing a check chain, something which should not be used without advice and training.

Things You Need to Buy

Before your dog arrives home you will need to buy a certain amount of equipment and it is a good idea to obtain it beforehand so that everything is to hand for the big event. In any case, you will not want to leave him to make a visit to the shops once he has arrived. This is not dissimilar to preparing for a new baby when you want everything to be perfect and just so right from the start.

Bowls

Your dog will require his own selection of feed and water bowls. Buy ones that are suitable for his size, and which are made of heavy stainless steel or ceramics. These are preferable as they will stay in one place as he feeds and will not move along the floor or be knocked over, which is a common failing with plastic ones. Always make sure that he has fresh water and clean bowls with each feed. Show the dog where his bowls are and keep them always in that place.

Collars and Leashes

It is vital that your dog is fitted with a collar straight away. For adult dogs there is a huge variety of collars available, from the most ornately worked leather to plain nylon. A dog's first collar should be of the buckled variety and should be fitted with an identity tag enabling him to be instantly returned to you should he stray. Even dogs fitted with an identity chip should have an identity tag as an extra precaution. The collar should fit so that it is comfortable, not so loose that it can slip over his head, and you should be able to comfortably fit two fingers between the collar and his neck.

Puppies have delicate skin, so find a collar which is soft and comfortable and not too expensive as they grow rapidly and may go through several before they are fully grown. In this case, the nylon variety is probably best as they are relatively chew-proof. In both cases you will also require a leash, as even a puppy who cannot yet go outside will need to be trained to walk while being restrained. Choose one of an appropriate length and width and which is long enough so that you do not have to stoop when walking. Make sure the leash is fitted with a secure clip fastener. There is no good or bad type of leash: choose the one that is the most comfortable for you. Your dog will inevitably try to chew it; discourage this rather than buying one of the chain variety which is unpleasant to hold, particularly in winter.

There are other types of collar and leashes which are used as methods of control. If your dog has a tendency to pull, it is preferable to teach him some manners and how to walk to heel. However, and as a last resort, these items have their uses. (See page 39 for more advanced methods of control.)

Extended Leashes

These are useful if you wish to give your dog a little more freedom if it is too dangerous for him to be allowed to run free or he is difficult to catch. They have comfortable plastic handles and easy controls which allow you to quickly let him out or reel him in as necessary.

Safety in the Home

Of utmost importance before bringing your dog or puppy home is to go over it and remove anything which may be dangerous or harmful, as well as taking steps to prevent your more precious items from getting broken. There is nothing a lively dog or puppy enjoys more than charging around, so remove valuable items of furniture, secure electric cables and unplug any electrical appliances, such as lamps, which may be pulled to the floor. Keep all harmful chemicals such as cleaning fluids, rat poison and insect sprays well out of reach and preferably locked away. Remember that puppies love to chew things up; don't leave shoes or bags lying around. Also place all house plants well out of reach; many are actually poisonous, so don't take any chances and remove them all.

Puppies have a natural urge

Leather Collar

Nylon Collar

Metal Identity Tag

Identity Barrel

Identity Chips

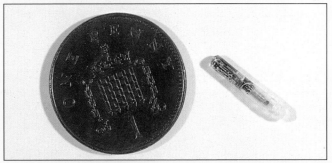

Recent technology has made it possible to have all your pets electronically tagged. A tiny microchip is painlessly injected into the loose skin around the animal's neck, where it should stay forever.

The chip contains a number which is logged into a central computer which has recorded the owner's name, address and telephone number. Have your dog chipped as a back-up to an identity disk. Above: The chip in relation to an English penny. Below: A dog being scanned, when a number will appear on the screen.

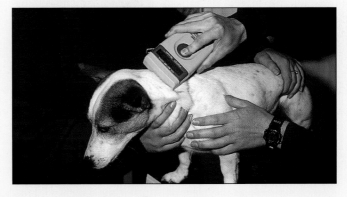

to chew. From the ages of 3 to 6 months, the adult teeth will begin to emerge, forcing the milk teeth out. This often causes pain and irritation as in human babies, so provide a selection of dog-proof toys of which there are many available. Dogs never seem to be free of the desire to chew, even when the adult teeth appear. Fortunately there are a variety of objects which they can legitimately chew up which include hard nylon toys and objects made from rawhide and sterilized bone. Provide plenty of these as it will help preserve your furniture. Also get some toys you can both play with, especially toys he can have fun pulling against; dogs love playing tug-of-war.

Safety in the Yard or Garden

There are some people who prefer their dogs to live outside, in which case they must ensure that there is a warm, water- and wind-proof kennel, and that it is ample enough. Place it in a

Left: This Weimaraner must be banned from the kitchen when cooking is in progress as such a large dog could easily put his paws onto a hotplate or pull scalding water over himself. Small dogs running around and getting under your feet are equally dangerous.

Below: Dogs like these are older and wiser and less likely to have accidents in the home. However, keep poisonous items well out of reach.

Opposite above: This Bouvier des Flandres is happily occupied in his own territory. His owner has made sure that the boundary fencing is secure so that he is perfectly safe from dangerous traffic.

Opposite below: This black Labrador is in extreme danger. His owner has not bothered to correctly secure his premises and the dog has managed to get out. Many hundreds of dogs are killed on the roads each year through the negligence of their owners, causing unnecessary heartache and potential injury to unfortunate motorists.

Safety in the home check list

Keep all poisonous plants out of reach

•

Keep poisonous household products locked away

•

Unplug appliances not in use and remove dangling cables

•

Remove small objects that could be swallowed or cause choking

Outdoor safety check list

Remove any poisonous plants

•

Ensure that boundaries are adequately fenced and that gates are secure

•

Fence ponds and cover swimming pools when not in use

•

Lock away garden tools and mowers

•

Lock away garden fertilizers and weedkillers

sheltered area, add plenty of warm washable bedding and a safe form of heating, if possible. Many thick-coated dogs thrive on outside conditions and some even prefer it, for example dogs with very dense coats designed to withstand harsh weather such as the Husky. This arrangement should not be used as an excuse to leave a dog on his own for hours on end; he requires just as much love and attention as a dog who lives indoors.

Your yard or garden must be adequately fenced to prevent your dog from roaming. Even in country areas where there appears to be little traffic, a fatal accident could still occur. A boundary fence of 4ft (1.2m) high for small dogs and 6ft (1.8m) for large dogs should be adequate, making sure that the fence is securely fixed at ground level. Dogs are keen diggers and talented burrowers, so make it a rule to check that fences and gates are secure on a regular daily basis.

Chapter Four
Training Your Dog

To make them accceptable in our homes, it is vital that all dogs are adequately house-trained and have learnt to be obedient. Dogs cannot be allowed to run riot making nuisances of themselves, and need to be taught what is acceptable and what is not. Young dogs need training from an early age, but it is not too late to teach adults who will be almost as quick to learn the error of their ways.

Handling

Over the years there will be many times when it is necessary to handle your dog, whether it be grooming him, cleaning his ears or paws, or giving him medicine. Consequently, it is a good idea to teach your puppy to accept being handled before it becomes actually necessary. Choose a time when he is relaxed and sleepy and practise lifting his ears, examining his paws, touching his body and opening his mouth. At the same time, talk to him in kindly tones and at the end offer him a treat. By doing this regularly from an

Above: This 10-week-old Jack Russell puppy should virtually be house-trained by now and is ready for simple training exercises.

Below: Handle your puppy or dog as much as possible; run your hands over his body and give him a health check, examining skin, paws, eyes, ears and teeth so that nothing is strange or frightening for him in the future.

Opposite
Above left: Your puppy needs to learn that playing with another dog is different from playing with you. Make him aware that snapping and biting are unacceptable forms of behaviour.

Above right: Tug-of-war is great fun and extremely good exercise.

Below: All dogs love chasing and retrieving games. This Labrador is happily playing hunt the boot.

early age, you will find that when examination is required, especially a veterinary one, he will not be unduly alarmed.

As he gets older, and to prevent your dog from becoming aggressive and possessive with his food, kneel beside him while he is feeding and gently cover the bowl, perhaps dropping in a morsel of something he particularly likes. He will begin to see the act of feeding as a shared experience and stop snapping at people and other animals at mealtimes.

Playing

All puppies love to play and it is an important part of their development. However, playing with a human being is rather different from playing with another dog and the puppy must be made aware of that important difference. He may try to bite you, and when this happens, tell him sharply NO, and if he become too uncontrollable put him in a room on his own until he calms down. When dogs play with one another, mock fighting instincts come to the fore, inherited from their lupine ancestry. This is fine among dogs but they must be made to understand what is acceptable when playing with you. If you watch two puppies at play you will notice that they see how hard they can bite without hurting one another; if one yelps with pain, the other will moderate his biting; if your puppy bites you, 'yelp' too and support this with an 'ouch' or NO. Don't strike or push him away, this will only excite him further. If he persists, shut him away on his own, for puppies don't like isolation and will soon learn to behave.

House-Training

Begin house-training a new puppy straight away. Even before you introduce him into his new home, show him a place outside in your yard or garden which is to be the area where he can urinate and defecate as it is, more than likely that, after a car journey, he may make use of it. If he doesn't, never mind, if he does, praise him warmly. From now on you will have to watch him closely to see what is on his mind. Puppies usually feel the urge to evacuate on waking and about 10–20 minutes after feeding. This is the optimum time to take him outside to the appointed place, especially if you see him circling or sniffing at the floor. Don't carry him out unless evacuation appears

Obedience

There are many different ways of training your dog to be obedient, but the most up-to-date and popular method is that of positive reinforcement. This relies heavily on the dog's natural wolf-like characteristics and the way wolves establish a natural pecking order within a social group.

Begin training puppies from day one. Because they are essentially pack animals, they will naturally look to a leader, and it is vital at this stage that *you* are recognized as such. Establish simple rules and boundaries for the puppy to follow. For example, try banning him from a particular room. If he attempts to enter, tell him NO in a firm voice. He will soon learn to comply with your demands as it is in his nature to obey, and there are many obedience activities which can be practised in the home using patience and kindness. Above all, remember that all good behaviour should be rewarded with praise and perhaps a treat. Don't overdo this aspect of training so that your dog gets bored; once he loses interest he will be far more difficult to train in future. Avoid trying anything too difficult to start with – you will only manage to confuse him.

If your dog is older, he may already understand some commands. Establish how much

imminent, let him follow you outside. Once the deed is done, praise him, make a fuss of him and tell him what a good boy he is. If he does soil indoors, which is inevitable as you cannot watch him constantly, unless you actually saw it happen, merely ignore it and quietly clean up. If you catch him in the act, tell him firmly NO and OUTSIDE and take him to the proper place to show him what you mean. Never strike or rebuke him after the event as this could easily develop into behavioural problems in the form of submissive urination.

At night, or if you have to go out, use the paper-training method below. If he performs in the night, when morning comes take him outside anyway, and go through the usual process of encouragement, then clean up the mess inside without fuss.

Paper-Training

For those who live in an apartment or cannot be with their pet all day, paper-training is another option. Teach him to evacuate by himself onto newspaper. First start by placing newspapers all over the floor when he will gradually develop a preference for a particular spot. This is the time to remove the newspapers, putting only a few in

that particular area. Hopefully, he will come to regard it as a spot where he can evacuate. Once this is established, and you wish him to go outside, gradually move the paper to the door and then eventually outside, leaving the paper there so that he can use it for a few times before you remove it completely. With a little luck, he will now associate going out with evacuation. When this happens, praise him every time he does the right thing.

In the case of an adult dog, you will usually be able to tell if he is house-trained. However, if he does have a few accidents, and he may because of the change in his routine, follow the same procedure as with a small puppy.

Above: When you bring your new puppy home, the first thing you should do is show him a place where he can evacuate. If he performs, praise him warmly.

Right: Reinforcement training involves backing up a command with consistent praise and the offer of an occasional treat. This Dalmation is accepting a treat for successfully completing the SIT command.

he already knows, reinforcing his successes with praise and rewards. On the other hand, he may have no idea what is required, or may have developed some bad habits. If this is the case, start from scatch as you would with a new puppy. With older dogs and puppies you will soon establish a way of training which is enjoyable to you both, which will further strengthen the bond of friendship between you.

Once you are both proficient in the basics of training and your puppy has had his vaccinations, it is time to take him out into the big wide world. Suddenly he will be bombarded by different sounds, smells and situations. His attention will at one be distracted and you may think

Right: It is important that every dog is well trained and has a responsive attitude, particularly in dangerous situations such as crossing a busy street.

Below: When a dog had worked particularly hard at his training, make a fuss of him and offer a reward in the form of a tasty treat. This way he will look forward to future training sessions.

that everything you have taught him has gone in one ear and out the other. Allow time for him to become accustomed to his strange new surroundings.

The best way of teaching your dog new commands is off the leash. However, don't take a new dog or puppy into an open space for the first time without one; spend the first few days walking him on it, making a start on his basic training by using commands such as HEEL, SIT and STAND. One useful command which can be performed anywhere is WATCH ME, maintaining eye contact with your dog for about 10 seconds while using the command. This is a useful basis for all training and brings to the dog's attention the fact that it is time for work. Use hand movements to reinforce your voice commands and reward with a treat as well as praise when he performs correctly. However, refrain from giving a treat every time; he needs to know that he must behave solely to please you, but always offer praise. Always end the training session with something he can do well and finish with praise and a game he really enjoys.

Once your dog is comfortable in his surroundings and you are confident that he will stay and not run off, you can let him off the leash. Find a quiet place with no distractions, and begin training using the commands you have already taught him at home or when on the leash. Keep the sessions short – no more than 15 minutes for a puppy, slightly more for an older dog. Any one person in your family can try his hand at training, but only one person at a time should issue commands as the dog may be confused and upset. Don't make the sessions too regular; be spontaneous. If he begins to equate going out with an obedience training session he may become difficult. Intersperse his training with lots of walks and games.

SIT

Getting your dog to sit at command is important and can be used when it is vital for him to stay still, for example, in a hazardous situation such as

preparing to cross a busy street.

It is obvious that dogs already know how to sit, but they need to be able to immediately react to the command to do so and this is easy to achieve, making use of the dog's natural conformation. Dogs have relatively inflexible spines, so the action of moving his head up will force him to sit down.

The process is best taught using a treat. Take the morsel between your finger and thumb, holding it slightly above his nose so that he can see and smell it. As you perform this action, say SIT. As the dog visually follows the treat, his head will come up and he will sit. Reward and praise him. Try this several times with and without a treat, but always with plenty of praise.

DOWN

This action is much more difficult, so take your time and be patient. Once again using a treat, ask the dog to SIT, then say DOWN, then hold the treat in front of the dog's nose and move it downwards with the dog's nose

following until it is between his front legs. This movement should make his back end slide down as he follows the treat. Once performed correctly, offer the treat and praise. If this method doesn't work, try pulling the treat from between his front feet forwards.

Above: Once your dog has mastered the command DOWN, you can teach him to roll over onto his back for a bit of fun.

Right: This chocolate Labrador Retriever has been taught to come to his owner, which he now does promptly and with enthusiasm.

STAND

To ask you dog to stand on command, begin by placing him in the lying position. Place a treat in front of his nose and move it up and away from him, using the command STAND. Finish by offering the treat and praising.

Now is the time to try combinations of all three commands, eventually with or without the treat until he is

proficient in all of them. An obedient dog who promptly adopts these positions on command will be easy to control in a multitude of situations, such as putting on or taking off the leash, making him stay put or asking him to lie down quietly.

COME

Teaching your dog to come is much more difficult but is one of the most important commands to establish and could be vital to his safety. It is not easy to teach because asking your dog to come to you is often for negative reasons, for example to come away from something which is interesting or great fun. So you may often be tempted to shout at him in frustration and admonish him when he eventually does decide to come.

HEEL

Prompt obedience is vital when you are walking a dog on the leash. There are many times when a dog cannot go unrestrained, so he will be required to walk quietly at heel, without pulling on the leash. Dogs which pull are extremely tiring on their owners' arms, and can damage themselves, producing distressing wheezing noises all the while. If you cannot make your dog come to heel on the leash you may both benefit from dog-training classes, or as a last resort you may wish to try out some of the various control collars (page 39).

It is usual in obedience training to bring your dog to heel on your left. Ask him to sit next to you and say WATCH ME, assuming that you have already taught him this command. Take a couple of steps forward, and if he has true eye contact with you he should move with you. If the dog stops when you stop, give him praise and perhaps a treat. Repeat the exercise, gradually increasing the number of paces.

Another method is to begin by making the dog sit. Hold a treat in each hand, placing your left hand near to him so that he can see and smell it and say HEEL as you move forward. Then raise this hand and, using the other hand, go through the SIT exercise, offering treats and praise. At times, repeat without the treat until he reacts to the command HEEL automatically.

Far left: A young girl is teaching her German Shepherd to stay. Anyone can partake in the training, but only one person should issue the commands at any one session to avoid confusion.

Left: This German Shepherd is walking perfectly to heel by his owner's side, making a walk in the park a pleasant experience for them both.

Below: It is most important to teach your dog to come to heel from a very early age as a dog the size of this Great Dane would be otherwise uncontrollable if he pulled on the leash.

STAY

Another useful command and one which could avert an accident in a hazardous situation. Once again, it is a difficult exercise and the aim is to make the dog 'stay' when the distance beween you both is at a minimum until he understands what you require. Only then, gradually increase the distance, rewarding with treats at first then with praise only.

First ask your dog to sit, then raise your open palm above his face and say STAY in a firm voice. Then gradually back away. If he manages to stay for more than 5 seconds, reward him. Repeat until you can move quite some distance away.

FETCH

This has no other purpose than to provide your dog with much needed exercise and save your own legs at the same time. Your dog's ability to 'fetch' proficiently depends largely on the breed type, retrievers having the ability inbred, with terriers finding it more difficult. Fetching is fun and all part of the throwing game. An easy way to teach your dog this trick is to throw a ball a short distance and say FETCH.

Follow these simple rules for happy and successful training:

Never use physical punishment

•

Never reprimand for not performing correctly

•

Keep the training session short and make it interesting with plenty of variety

•

Space training sessions irregularly so that the dog doesn't begin to anticipate

•

Initially, use tasty treats to help reinforce the command, reducing them to occasional use once proficiency is achieved

•

Give praise after every correctly performed task while ignoring those which are unsuccessful

•

End the training session on a good note. Finish with a task which your dog does well and praise him warmly, perhaps rewarding him with a treat. He is then more likely to remember that training sessions are fun

The Check Chain

Only to be used on a dog which persists in pulling at its leash, the check chain should never be used by an inexperienced handler. The effect of a sharp jerk, coupled with the word HEEL, for example, will hopefully correct the problem. It is a valuable aid for handlers who require their dogs to be on the leash for long periods, and prevents the dog from making the distressing 'wheezing' sound which results from dogs constantly pulling on a collar. Make sure the chain is correctly fitted as one that is incorrect could potentially result in strangulation. Always have an expert demonstrate the chain's use before buying one. There exists much controversy regarding the use of the check chain, and many insist that it should never be used in any circumstances. However, it is thought preferable to include it to warn people of the hazards rather than to ignore the matter altogether, when the inexperienced may be tempted to use one. REMEMBER: always remove the chain when letting the dog run free.

Opposite: Don't make your training session too long, and end it with a game. These three can't wait to chase a ball which is also a good time to teach your dog to retrieve.

Below: This Irish Setter is wearing a head-restraining collar which will hopefully stop him pulling. Don't use it if your dog suffers from neck or back problems. Make sure that the collar is correctly fitted and is not obstructing the airway.

When your dog picks it up, say COME and praise him when he does. To teach him to drop the ball on command, hold up a favourite toy and say DROP; the dog should relinquish the ball in favour of the toy when you should praise him and throw the toy. Repeat until he gets the idea, gradually eliminating the toy.

Training Aids

It has been mentioned that when teaching your dog to come to heel you may encounter difficulties. Listed here are some artificial methods of control. However, they should only be used when all other avenues have been explored and found unsuccessful.

Slip- & Half-Check Chains

These are useful for dogs which pull on the collar to a lesser extent. They are ideal for small or delicate dogs and are much kinder than the check chain. They are also much safer, especially when utilized by the heavy-handed. They are not as effective as the check chain but rather more preferable.

Head-Restraining Collars

These look much the same as a horse's bridle, but of course without the bit. The idea is that when the dog pulls, its head will turn inwards which significantly reduces his power to pull. It is preferable to seek advice from your vet before fitting your dog with one of these as they are not suitable for some breeds of dog and can damage the eyes; also dogs which are susceptible to neck injuries should not be fitted with one. They are effective in stopping a dog from pulling, but are of little use as a training aid to correct the problem, as the restraining collar merely blocks the desire to pull rather than training the dog not to do it.

Harnesses

Harnesses may be useful when a conventional collar is causing the dog breathing problems and soreness from constant pulling. However, it will not cure the problem – if anything it is more likely to compound it.

Spiked Collars

An unfortunately named piece of equipment, when used to control a pulling dog, the 'spikes', which are in fact blunt prongs, tighten as the dog pulls, pinching the skin of the neck. It is not a pleasant form of control and its use is banned in some countries.

Unwanted Behaviour

To understand why your dog is behaving in an unacceptable manner you will need to find the root cause of the problem. Understanding why he is misbehaving is the first step to finding a cure. Striking the dog or shouting at him is likely to make matters worse. Be calm and patient and eventually the problem will be solved. There follows some of the more common forms of unwanted behaviour. For more complex problems you may require the help of your vet or an animal behaviourist.

Aggression

The most serious problem, even in the smallest of breeds, is the dog which bites and its bite can cause serious damage. Other aggressive traits are some types of barking, growling, baring of the teeth, and lunging or snapping. A prelude to aggression is that the dog may stand very still and square with an alert expression on his face with his hackles raised. (The hackles are a ridge of hair which rises from the nape of the neck and trails off down the spine.) Aggressive behaviour towards other dogs is common in unneutered males, so the obvious solution if you wish him to interact happily with other dogs is to have your own dog neutered, preferably before puberty. Other causes of aggression are fear and nervousness (often as a result of previous ill-treatment), and these forms are often the most dangerous as they are directed at people. If your dog has attacked or bitten anyone, be it a member of your family or a stranger, you must tackle the problem immediately. Ask your vet, he may be able to recommend a

suitable animal behaviourist who specializes in this type of aberration. Happily, by correctly training your puppy from an early age you are less likely to encounter aggressive behaviour later on. We have already discussed how you have gradually established yourself as your dog's pack leader by handling him; also practise taking food away from him, then returning it with praise. This will stop him being aggressive at mealtimes. You can do the same with a favourite bone or toy. You should also approach your pet when he is sleeping, waking him up gently so that he is not upset when at his most vulnerable.

Accustomize your puppy to strangers and other dogs as soon as possible. Socializing early on will make him feel more confident with strangers in the future and less likely to be aggressive through fear or uncertainty.

Never physically reprimand a dog; this is more likely to make the situation worse. Instead, tell him firmly NO and couple this with a stern and disapproving look.

Above: Aggressive behaviour just cannot be tolerated in any circumstances. If your dog begins to show vicious tendencies, contact your vet who will be able to recommend an animal behaviourist to help solve the problem. Separate aggressive dogs from children and keep dogs muzzled in public places.

Opposite
Above left: Excessive barking is a nuisance, not only to you but may also drive your neighbours to distraction. It is possible to train your dog not to bark, or if this fails there are products available to help alleviate the problem. If your dog is prone to barking, don't leave him outside on his own – this will only serve to exacerbate the problem.

Above right: Teach your dog to greet visitors pleasantly without jumping up. A large dog could easily topple a person over in his exuberance.

Below: There are various training methods designed to discourage your dog from jumping up. However, there are times when you may want him to do this. If this is the case, train him to do so only on command.

When new people come to the house, utilize your dog's new-found obedience skills. Ask him to sit, and get the stranger to give him a treat and a pat. This way a visitor will be someone to be welcomed rather than feared.

Don't leave your dog tied up in a confined space for too long; because he is a territorial animal he may well try to defend his space in an aggressive manner. If he does begin to show signs of aggression or if you have just acquired an older dog and are unsure how he will react, never let him off the leash until you are happy that his problems have been sorted out, and never think that your dog will grow out of aggessive behaviour; in fact, the problem is likely to become worse, so tackle it straight away and seek any professional advice you may require.

Muzzles

Much controversy surrounds the use of these, many countries having made it illegal for some dangerous breeds, such as the Pit Bull Terrier, to go out in public places without one. However, many experts are convinced that they actually make the problem of aggression worse, causing the dog frustration and discomfort. Great care should always be taken when de-muzzling a dog as the muzzle will tend to make him momentarily more aggressive. Always consult your vet before muzzling a dog as there may be other kinder and more effective ways of curbing him, such as re-training, as mentioned above.

Excessive Barking

All dogs bark from time to time – it is the canine form of communication. It would be unkind to totally deter a dog from barking as it is often a sign that he loves life and wants someone to play with him.

an entirely different matter, as a frail person or child could quite easily be pushed over and frightened quite badly. If you want your dog to jump up as a trick, teach him by command using the various methods outlined in this chapter; but if you want him to stop the habit, rush towards him; this will throw him off balance and distract him from his purpose. Alternatively you could try the SIT and STAY commands. Another ploy, when you arrive home, is to ignore the dog until he has calmed down, then make a fuss of him with praise and a treat and hopefully he will begin to relinquish his anti-social behaviour. Once control is established, keep to the routine, letting him know that he will get no attention until he is sitting calmly. If you cannot stop him from jumping up, keep him on a leash and pull him down, or try a head-restraining collar. This gives you fuller control of the neck, allowing you to pull him away more effectively without causing damage.

Radio-Controlled Collars

These should only be used as a last resort and only on the advice of your vet or a qualified animal behaviourist. They are designed for dogs who are constantly escaping and out of control. The dog's unruly behaviour is in fact curbed by a mild electric shock. There is a great deal of controversy as to the ethics surrounding their use, but they are becoming ever more popular and many people swear by them. It is claimed that once the dog has had one or two shocks he will establish the parameters of his area and stay within it, while others stress that such an unnatural form of control could cause a dog severe psychological damage.

There are similar versions designed to stop constant barking, which once again should only be used as a remedy of last resort. There is a much kinder method called the olfactory collar; when the dog barks, the collar emits a squirt of citronella oil which is activated by a microphone. The dog soon links barking with what is to him an unpleasant odour and stops the irritating habit.

Jumping Up

Some dogs have the annoying habit of jumping up at their owners as well as strangers as they are greeting them or when something has particularly excited them. While small dogs do little harm, apart from their dirty paws and scratchy claws damaging clothing, it can nonetheless be extremely tiresome. However, a large dog is

Digging up the Garden

Digging is a deeply-rooted part of a dog's instinctual behaviour and many have actually been bred for the purpose; for instance, terriers are sometimes required to dig for small animals which burrow underground while many dogs feel the need to dig a hole to bury a bone. This goes back to their lupine ancestry when wolves would bury their kill to save it for another day.

Once again, try to get to the root of the problem. If he persists in digging in one spot you may be able to train him to LEAVE by command, using treats to distract him, or there may be a smell which is stimulating him. Try to find the source and if it is in one particular area you could try replacing the old soil with new, or planting some large shrubs to distract him from the spot. He may be digging to make a cool place to lie down in; if this is so, make a shady spot for him elsewhere or keep him indoors on hot days. However, he may just like digging as a hobby when you are better off giving in and making him his own special place in which to dig, perhaps in

the form of a sandpit, or an area of bark chippings. Encourage him to bury his favourite toys there; he will soon latch on to the fact that this is his very own play area. If he persists in digging in a no-go area, reprimand him with a firm NO and return him to the place where he is allowed to dig; start by flicking at the sand which may stimulate him to begin digging there again, and when he does, praise him for it.

Stealing

Puppies and older dogs love to hold objects in their mouths and may run off with your precious possessions. Firstly, whenever possible, don't leave portable objects of value lying around. However, if your dog has grabbed something he shouldn't have, don't shout at him as he will probably run off with it; equally, don't chase him as he will immediately think that you are playing a game and you will have great difficulty in getting him to come back. The most effective way is to crouch down beside him and offer a treat, followed by the command DROP, when he will most likely relinquish your

property in favour of the treat. You can practise this with him using worthless objects so that he learns to drop them on command from an early age.

Above: Attacking the mail may be an act of defence, the mail being regarded as an intruder. To protect your letters, install either an external post box or fix a basket over the letter box to catch the mail before it hits the ground.

Left: The instinct to dig is strong in most dogs and very difficult to cure. The best course of action is to provide him with his own place in your garden where he is allowed to dig. Bury his favourite things in it to encourage him.

Opposite: Cure or prevent your dog from stealing and running away with your belongings by teaching him the FETCH and DROP commands.

Chapter Five
Feeding and Exercise

Correct feeding is the most important aspect of dog care and is vital if your dog is to stay healthy and happy. As previously mentioned, there are some similarities between people and dogs. They, like us, are omnivores, which means that they require both meat and vegetables in their diet which must also contain the correct levels of carbohydrates, vitamins and minerals to keep them well. Dogs also require as much water as they can drink, which is an important aid to digestion. Like us, they require feeding according to size, shape, age and lifestyle. The diets of a sheepdog working on a farm and a pampered pet living in an apartment will be considerably different. The diet of a pregnant female will also vary, as will that of puppies which need higher levels of nutrients for healthy growth. It is very important that

you don't overfeed; you may think you are being kind by offering big meals and tasty treats; however, the opposite is true and will inevitably end in obesity and even illness.

There are many different varieties of proprietary foods on the market, all of which contain the correct levels of minerals, vitamins and other additives which go towards creating a well balanced diet for a dog.

Canned Foods

These come in a variety of brands and range considerably in price and quality. They contain approximately 75 per cent water mixed with various meat and fish products and cereals. Needless to say, they are very convenient. However, because they produce quite low energy levels you would have to feed a large dog quite a lot, which would make them very expensive. For larger

dogs it is advisable to mix them with dried food to bulk them up and add more energy value.

All-Meat Canned Foods

As the name suggests, these contain only meat and to provide your dog with the levels of energy he requires you would have to feed him a large amount which would produce an unhealthy, unbalanced diet. Consequently, they should always be combined with mixers.

Semi-Moist Foods

These have a much higher concentration with only 15–30 per cent water content allowing you to feed lesser quantities. They contain meat, vegetables, cereals, fats and sugars and are easy to digest and very palatable. They come in a huge range and are a popular method of feeding. They can be stored without refrigeration but are rather

expensive. However, they are particularly suitable for small, fussy dogs. Not to be fed to dogs which are diabetic as they contain high levels of sugar.

Dry Foods

These contain only about 10 per cent water and have a high-energy content. However, they mostly contain cereal so should only be used as mixers, or as a supplement with canned foods to provide a well balanced diet. These foods contain all the important proteins; for example, meat, bone meal and soy flour, but have little smell and are therefore not very palatable. Some are used as mixers to boost the energy content of canned foods. The advantages are that they can be stored in large quantities and are cheaper than other foods; however, don't keep them past their sell-by date as they will have lost most of

Fresh with Biscuit

Dry

Semi-Moist

Canned

their vitamin content. Be careful when feeding these as it is easy to give too much, which could lead to obesity.

Home Cooking

It is quite possible to feed your dog food which you have prepared and cooked yourself at home. However, it is most important that it contains the correct dietary requirements and there are various recipe books on the subject. Don't attempt this course of action without advice as you could deprive your dog of all-important nutrients.

It is vital that your dog is fed the correct levels of proteins, fats, carbohydrates, vitamins, minerals and fibre, as well as water.

Proteins

Vital for development, a dog's ability to digest protein varies. In the form of meat, 90 per

Opposite: Your dog's eating habits and the amount of exercise he is given are directly linked. He will require a well balanced diet containing proteins, carbohydrates, fats, vitamins and minerals.

Above: This working Border Collie requires very much higher levels of energy foods when compared to a less active dog.

Right: Make sure that your dog always has plenty to drink. Water is important to digestion as well as cooling down and re-hydrating the system on a hot day.

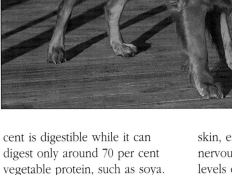

cent is digestible while it can digest only around 70 per cent vegetable protein, such as soya. However, feeding high levels of vegetable protein can cause bowel upsets.

Fats

Fats in the form of fatty acids are a vital part of the diet and are essential to a dog's well-being as deficiencies can cause

skin, ear problems and nervousness. They offer high levels of energy which means that the dog has to digest less protein which reduces the work the liver and kidneys have to do. The dog can digest virtually 100 per cent of fats.

Carbohydrates

These are the highest form of energy in the dog's diet and

consist of starches, sugars and cellulose. To provide your dog with the required levels of carbohydrates, feed boiled potatoes or rice, with dried foods and mixers to a lesser extent. Some canned foods have between 12 and 15 per cent carbohydrate while fresh meat and fish have none at all, so it is important when feeding these that you include a mixer which contains some carbohydrate.

Fibre

High-fibre diets have become very popular with the human population and have proved to be beneficial, and this also applies to dogs. Add about 5 per cent fibre to the total diet which is what you will find added to meat and cereal-based dog foods and biscuit-based mixers. Fibre is an important aid to digestion and speeds up the movement of food through the gut, thus reducing the risk of bowel complaints such as diarrhoea and flatulence. It also helps absorb toxins, which are by-products of digestion, which as a consequence ease stress on the liver. It is also an excellent idea to increase the amount of fibre fed to obese dogs, filling them up without adding to their

Above: Growing puppies require careful feeding for correct growth and development. Overfeeding can cause a good deal of damage to a young dog so ask your vet or breeder to suggest correct feeding guidelines.

Right: Feed your dog his own meal when you have yours; this will discourage him from begging at mealtimes. Paws on the table are not to be encouraged.

Opposite: A dog likes nothing better than to gnaw on a big juicy bone. These benefit the teeth and exercise the jaws. Only give him a knuckle bone as this won't splinter; don't give cooked bones. Other alternatives are hide chews and treated bones available from feed suppliers.

Golden Rules of Feeding

Never overfeed your dog

•

Feed according to size, age and lifestyle

•

Feed a well-balanced diet which contains correct levels of proteins, carbohydrates, fats, fibre, vitamins and minerals

•

Always provide a constant supply of fresh water

•

Don't constantly feed fresh food without taking advice, otherwise your dog may go short of vital nutrients

Approximate energy requirements

Average weight of dog		Energy required (kcals per day)
sml breeds	2kg (2.2lbs)	230
	5	450
	10	750
med breeds	15	1010
	20	1250
	25	1470
Lge breeds	30	1675
	35	1875
	40	2070

Approx. contents of branded dog foods

Food	Pr	Car	Fa	Wa	Kc
Dry (complete)	22%	51%	7%	15%	3.4
Semi-moist	19%	38%	10%	26%	3.0
Canned (complete)	8%	12%	5%	73%	1.0
Canned (total meat)	9.5%	1.5%	5%	82%	1.3
Biscuit	10%	69.9%	6.1%	8.4%	3.5

Pr=Protein   **Car**=Carbohydrate   **Fa**=Fat
Wa=Water   **Kc**= Kcals per gram

weight problem. It is also useful for diabetic dogs as fibre absorbs glucose.

Vitamins and Minerals

As in all animals, the correct balance of vitamins and minerals is vital for the proper functioning of the body. They are also an important factor in the prevention of disease. Ready-prepared dog foods already contain a careful balance of these elements to provide all that a dog needs. Particularly important are calcium and phosphate, which play an important part in the dog's development, including the formation of bones and healthy teeth. If you are feeding fresh food you will have to make sure that you are providing your dog with enough minerals and vitamins. Many are contained in dried foods which can be added as a supplement.

Energy

Feed your dog according to the amount of energy used. Some dogs are extremely athletic and have a fast metabolic rate. These will require foods with a higher energy content. However, others may be far less active, in which case they will require much less food. Never be tempted to

overfeed a growing dog, even a large one. Overeating can cause growth abnormalities and even shorten a dog's life. The chart above provides a rough guide to the energy levels in the form of calories required for dogs of different sizes. However, this should be increased or decreased according to activity, age, pregnancy and lactation. All

ready-prepared dog foods will have a feeding chart on the packaging. Use it as an important guide but watch out for signs of obesity and reduce the feed accordingly. A sign that you are overfeeding is that your dog may vomit or develop diarrhoea. In extreme cases, consult your vet who will plan a special diet for him.

Feeding Time

Most adult dogs only require one meal a day and most people prefer to feed this in the evening. A good idea is to let it coincide with your own evening meal which will deter your dog from begging at table. Some dogs with an evening meal inside them cannot last the night without having to go outside; in

Above: The most effective form of exercise is to allow your dog to run free. Before letting him off the leash, make sure that he has been trained to obey the commands COME and STAY. Be aware of local by-laws; for example some beaches ban dogs totally or during certain months of the year. Don't let your dog off in the presence of people or other dogs if he is at all aggressive.

Opposite: Select a time to feed your dog and stick to it so that he has a regular routine. Some dogs are quite happy with one meal a day while smaller dogs may not be able to eat a whole meal in one sitting, and you will need to split it into two or even three.

which case, feed earlier in the day. Smaller dogs may not be able to eat a meal in one sitting, so divide the amount into two and feed half morning and evening. Puppies and lactating mothers require a different regimen of feeding. Your vet will give advice here.

Always feed your dog in the same place, offering clean bowls with every meal, and also fresh water. Place the bowls on an easy-to-clean surface such as the kitchen floor. Remove any uneaten food immediately and discard.

Don't be tempted to feed your dog titbits from the table or give him snacks between meals. This will encourage begging and scrounging and is most annoying as well as likely to make him fat. You may feed small treats when training, but only in moderation, and you can break them up into smaller pieces to make them go further. There are dog treats available on the market for this purpose, but remember that they are

fattening. The best option is a dog biscuit, which is high in carbohydrate but low in fat.

Bones

A meat bone can provide a dog with hours of pleasure as well as exercising the jaws and cleaning the teeth. Offer a raw knuckle bone as this is unlikely to splinter. Avoid cooked bones, especially chicken; these will splinter and could cause severe internal damage.

Exercise

Exercise and feeding go hand-in-hand and your dog's level of exercise will depend on his size, age and breeding. It is not necessarily the case that large dogs require more exercise, in fact a Jack Russell Terrier requires more exercise than a Great Dane.

Walking your dog and playing games with him is not only beneficial to you both but is part of the joy of dog ownership. Exercise plays a vital part in your dog's well-being,

and will keep him fit, healthy and happy. A dog which is confined to the house all day will become lethargic, dull and fat; he may also develop behavioural problems such as excessive barking and destructive tendencies.

We have already discussed the wisdom of acquiring a breed of dog which suits your needs, so if you personally cannot walk far, you should have chosen a dog which requires a small amount of exercise.

All dogs require daily exercise, be it a walk round the block twice a day for the more sedate breeds, to a ramble in the countryside or a strenuous game in the park for more energetic types. Working breeds, such as sheepdogs, will obviously get all the exercise they need in the course of their working lives. Before you begin any form of exercise, especially if you have acquired an older dog, it is a good idea to have your vet check him over first as he may be suffering from a

permitted to be off the leash.

Bring a ball or frisbee for him to chase, or arrange to meet up with other dog owners so that all the dogs can run around and play together; this is good, strenuous exercise for them, great fun to watch, and is a way of enabling dogs to interact socially with one another.

If you are yourself a keen walker, nothing could be better than to take your dog for a long walk in the countryside. He will love sniffing about and will probably cover three times your distance as he runs backwards and forwards, searching out interesting sights and smells. Follow the country code: don't let your dog anywhere near livestock. If there are notices demanding that dogs be kept leashed, obey them. If you are out for a long time, make sure you bring some water with you and that he does not overheat.

Left: Walking is good gentle exercise and is ideal for older and unfit people as well as animals.

Below: A good ball game is a dog's idea of heaven and they will happily play for hours, saving your legs in the process. Teach him to retrieve and you won't have to move at all!

Opposite
Above: Dog owners should have respect for others and remove their dogs' excreta from public areas. Many places have special bins for the purpose and there are a number of different bags and scoops on the market. Dog faeces is not only unpleasant, it can cause actual harm to young children and pregnant mothers.

Below: When out in the countryside, only use marked paths and follow the country code. Don't let your dog off the leash if there are any livestock or wild animals about.

heart problem or stiff joints which energetic exercise might aggravate.

Walking

This is an excellent form of exercise for both you and your dog as the gentle movement tones muscles, and is beneficial to heart and lungs. If your dog is unfit, start with a short walk of no longer than 15 minutes and build it up slowly as he becomes fitter. Old or ill dogs will still benefit from some exercise – ask your vet's advice.

Playing and Running Free

If you live in an area where there are lots of people around, keep you dog on the leash and if there is nowhere to let him run free you will have to walk further to give him the exercise he requires. Young and active dogs really do need to run free, but only attempt this if your dog obeys your commands, you are sure that he is not aggressive, and that dogs are actually

clean up after your dog as its excrement can be extremely harmful, particularly to children and pregnant women, as well as being unpleasant and anti-social when it adheres to your shoes. There are various products available, from elaborate scoops to simple bags and most public areas are provided with a special disposal bin for the purpose. So use it.

Although not relevant to the presence of dogs in public places, you should also be aware of rules regarding tail docking and ear cropping which is banned in the U.K. but widely practised in the United States. While tail docking is not actually banned, it is increasingly being discouraged.

Watch out for hazards such as deep holes, barbed wire and watch that your dog doesn't eat anything which is potentially poisonous.

Another form of exercise is to take him jogging with you, but use common sense; make sure that he is fit enough, keep to soft ground to save his paw pads and avoid doing it in hot weather. Don't take a puppy with you which is under 6 months old as serious damage could be done to soft bones.

Be Responsible

Before taking your dog to a public place you should familiarize yourself with any local regulations and laws regarding the right to keep a dog. Some countries insist on a dog being licenced, others have restrictions regarding dogs in public places. Be aware also of laws concerning certain breeds which may require muzzling and in the U.K. some breeds are totally banned.

Finally, remember to always

Chapter Six
Grooming

You do not groom your dog solely for cosmetic reasons, it is an important aspect of his overall care. Regular grooming helps to keep the coat clean and the skin in good condition. It also provides an excellent opportunity to check for ticks, fleas, and other abnormalities.

All dogs require grooming to a greater or lesser extent. It is obvious that long-haired types will need more attention, but breeds with shorter coats will benefit from a brisk grooming, if only to bring out the natural shine of the coat.

Long-haired varieties such as Newfoundlands, Afghans and Poodles require at least one hour's grooming a day, so unless you are prepared to put in this amount of work, don't buy a long-haired breed. For those who wish to show their dogs, professional clipping and grooming may be required at extra expense.

A dog should eventually grow to enjoy grooming sessions, having been shown from an early age that it is pleasant by having a soft brush run gently over his body, or use the handling techniques on page 32.

Start off the grooming session with an examination to satisfy yourself that your dog is healthy; check that his skin is clean and free from dandruff, and

Opposite

Top: Long-haired dogs require daily grooming. This German Shepherd is having his tail brushed.

Below left: Short-haired dogs are easy to keep clean and tidy. This German Pointer has a lovely, lustrous coat.

Below right: Regular grooming helps keep the coat and skin clean and gives the owner an opportunity to check for skin problems. This little dog is thoroughly enjoying all the attention.

Below: Old English Sheepdogs have a thick, dense and curly coat. They require daily grooming to keep knots at bay. It is a good idea to give him a further quick groom after exercise to remove the worst of the tangles.

if there is evidence of fleas (see page 62). Check that the body is free from lumps and abrasions, and that the ears are free from discharge and that the eyes are clear and bright. If he begins to object, offer a treat and praise him warmly.

Then, using a wide-toothed comb, gently remove the excess dirt and knots, finishing off with a suitable brush. Then, using separate pieces of cotton wool moistened with water, gently remove any discharge from the eyes, and clean and remove dirt from ears and nose. You will also need to clean the teeth. Do this using either a flannel face-cloth or a toothbrush and some canine toothpaste.

Don't use your own toothpaste as it is strictly unsuitable. Finally, check to see if the nails need clipping; the need for this will vary according to the amount of exercise the dog takes, but may be necessary every few weeks or so.

The Coat

Dogs have varying types of coat, and each one requires a different type of grooming.

Long with an Undercoat –
Seen in breeds such as the Afghan and Samoyed. The coat should be brushed thoroughly forward and then back; once the knots are removed, tackle the fluffy undercoat with a comb.

Silky – As in the Yorkshire and West Highland Terriers. Brush daily, trimming or stripping out the loose older hair every three months.

Smooth – As in Dobermans and Labradors. Most dirt will brush off easily. Use a comb and bristle brush and a hound glove to give shine and improve the circulation.

Curly – As in Poodles. This type of dog never sheds its coat, so mats and knots will develop very quickly and remain there unless extra attention is paid to them. Groom daily using a brush and comb. A regular professional clip will go a long way to making your task easier.

Wiry – Groom twice a week. Coat can be stripped or clipped to make it more manageable.

Equipment

There are a variety of brushes and combs available; choose those which are suitable for your dog's coat. Other tools you may require are stripping combs, shears and scissors which are used to thin and trim the coat. Don't use electric clippers unless you have received training in their use. To prolong the life of your equipment, clean it thoroughly after use.

Combs

You will require two of these, one wide-toothed with rounded edges and ends to protect the

Nail-Clipping

You will need to attend to your dog's nails regularly, so invest in a good quality pair of clippers. The most suitable types are the ones which cut sharply like a guillotine as opposed to those which merely crush the nail. These can cause a great deal of pain, making nail-clipping a dreaded experience. When clipping, be extremely cautious. If your dog has a pale nail you will easily be able to see the quick and a pink area coming down the centre. If you cut through this, it will bleed and be very painful. So cut well away from this. If your dog has black nails, take off only the thin tip at the end.

Above: The Chow Chow has a very thick dense coat wich needs regular grooming to maintain its attractive fluffy appearance.

Right: The Basset only requires a quick going over with a bristle brush. Make sure that you clean under his ears at least once a week.

Opposite
Above: The Norfolk Terrier had a thick medium-length coat which is waterproof and requires regular grooming. Particular attention is needed during moulting.

Below: This Irish Setter has a beautiful russet, medium to long coat. The hair is fine and silky and can easily become knotted so will need to be groomed daily.

skin, and a fine-toothed version. These come in either plastic or metal which will obviously last longer but are likely to be more expensive. The wide-toothed comb is first used to break up mats and tangles and remove large patches of mud. The finer comb is used on the undercoat to remove loose hair. Don't tug the comb through the hair; if you meet with resistance, remove the comb and gently work on the knots little-by-little using your fingers and the comb. The fine comb will also help you to detect the presence of fleas.

Bristle Brush
The brush does most of the work and should be used after all the knots have been removed. It can also be used to give a dog which is well groomed a once-over to tidy the

Handy container to keep your grooming tools in

Carder

Wide-Toothed Comb

Fine-Toothed Comb

Hound Glove

Bristle Brush

coat. For long-haired dogs, the brush should have bristles which are long enough to penetrate the coat as far as the skin, thus preventing matting of the undercoat. For shorter-haired breeds, use a shorter-bristled brush. You are advised to use a brush composed of natural bristles as the synthetic varieties can cause static as well as damaging the hair and skin.

When brushing a long-haired dog, brush against the 'lie' of the coat using short strokes. Work on small patches at a time and don't tackle the whole coat by brushing in the wrong direction as you may damage the hair.

When brushing a medium-coated dog, pay particular attention to the quarters as it is here that much of the loose hair accumulates.

Carder

This is a rectangular board on which short bent-wire teeth are mounted. Its purpose is to remove the loose undercoat on shorter-haired varieties but can also be used on long-haired dogs by working the carder into the skin, then twisting away through the hair to the surface.

Hound Glove

Used solely on short-haired dogs such as Labradors, it is composed of short bristles, rubber bumps or wire teeth and you can wear it like a glove, working over the dog to remove loose hair and add shine.

Bathing

By our standards dogs are dirty creatures: they like nothing better than to snuffle through mud, and enjoy rolling in unspeakable things with terrible odours, making them offensive and unwelcome in the house. Time for a bath. If your dog is a persistent roller he will obviously require bathing more often; however, the rule is not to bath more than once a month unless it is really necessary. Only use a

shampoo which has the correct pH balance suitable for dogs, and not intended for people when it will dry out the skin causing irritation and flaky patches. Avoid bathing working dogs too much as shampoo strips the fur of its natural oils which are important for waterproofing the coat.

Summer is the ideal time to wash your dog outside using a garden hose and he will probably enjoy being cooled off on a hot day. In cooler conditions, either wash him in the bath, or the sink if he is small. Before bathing, and especially if he is long-haired, give him a thorough grooming, removing all knots, then place a wad of cotton wool in each ear if he will let you. Before placing a dog in the bath, prepare the water. It is best to use a shower hose, making sure that the water is lukewarm. Remove his collar and lift him gently into the bath (you may need a helper at first to hold him steady). Using the hose, wet him thoroughly, avoiding the ears, eyes and nose. Apply the shampoo, rubbing it in well, and include the legs, tail and paw pads. Wash the head carefully. Rinse off thoroughly, removing every trace of shampoo. Before he can shake himself everywhere, cover him with a towel, dry him vigorously, and leave him somewhere warm to dry, or in summer put him in the garden in the sunshine. You may use a hair drier if your dog will tolerate it, but don't hold it too close as you may burn him.

Above left: Necessary grooming tools include wide- and fine-toothed combs, a hound glove, bristle brush and a carder. Look after your tools by keeping them clean and free from hair.

Left: This little dog is having a final groom with a bristle brush before being treated with a flea spray. Regular brushing and combing helps reduce the incidence of fleas.

Opposite: Groomed, beautiful and ready for the show ring.

Chapter Seven
Travelling

The dog as part of a family (pack) thrives on human companionship, so it is hardly surprising that he loves going on holiday with his owner. This is perfectly possible as long as you make the proper preparations. If you are planning to provide your own accommodation, i.e. in tents or a trailer, then there is no problem. However, if you are staying at a hotel you will need to check in advance that dogs are allowed. Many will welcome them in all rooms, while others will allow dogs only in the bedrooms; if you are planning long evenings out you will need to make sure that somebody can sit with him.

There are times, however, when you will need to weigh up the pros and cons of taking your dog on holiday at all; does he get travel sick? Will he end up in a crate in the hold of a plane? Is the climate at your destination very hot or are you planning outings to restaurants and theatres in the evenings? If so, he may be happier staying with a relative or being boarded out in kennels, especially where quarantine regulations exist.

If you decide to take him with you abroad, you will need to take a supply of drinking water from home. Dogs suffer

from stomach upsets as well as human beings, so unless you want to give him expensive bottled water, bring your own. (For the same reason, bring a supply of his usual brand of food with you.) Make sure that all vaccinations are up-to-date, check with your vet to see if further inoculations are required and take proof of vaccination with you. Make sure that the dog's identification tag is well marked and have an identichip fitted as an extra precaution. Bring his licence, if necessary,

and his own bed for comfort as well as his favourite toys and grooming tools.

Travelling by Car

Make sure that your dog is adequately restrained, either in a crate or in a seat belt designed for dogs. Don't let him run loose around the car; he could distract the driver and in the event of a crash be badly injured or killed.

If he gets travel sick, don't feed him until the journey is over. Stop for regular breaks,

Top: Some dogs love being in cars, others don't. Get your puppy used to travelling from an early age, even if it is just a trip around the block. Don't feed bad travellers immediately before you set off and give him a good walk beforehand when hopefully he will go to sleep.

Above: Make sure that your dog is well restrained while travelling in the car, either with a harness, as illustrated, or secured in a crate.

Above left: Never leave your dog alone in the car. Even on dull days he may be overcome by heat.

taking him for short walks to stretch his legs and allowing him to urinate or have a drink.

Don't for any reason leave your dog alone in the car if you value his health and safety. Many have been stolen, and others have become overheated and died causing heartbreak and suffering to their thoughtless owners. Even on a cool day, a dog left for any length of time confined to a car may be overcome by heatstroke. (If you see a dog left in a car and it appears to be in distress, call the police straight away.)

Travelling by Air

This is quite a traumatic experience for a dog and should only be undertaken if really necessary. Some airlines will allow a small dog to travel in an approved carrier under the seat, while larger animals will have to be put in a crate in the hold. If you are travelling by air you will need to book early as space allotted to animals is limited. Try to reserve places on a non-stop flight and travel in the coolest part of the day if possible.

Tranquillizers

If your dog is a bad traveller your vet may prescribe tranquillizers which are not the perfect solution as breathing difficulties may occur. A better idea is to take your dog for a good walk or run which will tire him out so that he will sleep throughout the journey.

Boarding Kennels

If you are going away and you don't want to take your dog with you, you will have to find alternative accommodation for him. The best option is for him to stay with a relative or friend with whom he is on good terms; alternatively, have someone move into your house. Don't leave him at home on his own, even with someone coming in to feed and exercise

Left: Fun for all the family! This dog has clearly found his sea legs. If you do decide to take your dog boating, particularly at sea, make sure that he is fitted with a harness or lifejacket.

Below: Never leave your dog at home alone for long periods of time as he is a sociable animal and may fret or resort to destructive behaviour. This black Labrador is wistfully looking out of the cat-flap, presumably in the hope that his owner may soon appear.

him; he will be very lonely on his own and may become destructive, causing damage or even behaving in a manner likely to endanger himself.

The other option is to lodge him in a boarding kennel, and many are excellent. The best way to find one is on the recommendation of a friend or your vet. Take a look at the establishment before you book the dog in; there should be someone living on the premises at all times as well as quick access to a vet in emergencies and an adequate place in which to exercise the animals. The kennels themselves should be warm and dry and not too cramped and the food should be of good quality. Once you are satisfied that all is well, book your dog in. You will need to do this well in advance of your holiday, particularly if you are planning on travelling at holiday peak periods. A reputable kennel will not take your dog unless he is fully vaccinated, so make sure that these are up-to-date. When you drop him off, provide him with his own bedding and some toys to make him feel at home.

Chapter Eight
Health Matters

If you feed your dog a well-balanced diet, give him plenty of love, play and exercise, you can expect him to live a long and healthy life. You can also save him from many serious diseases by taking preventive measures in the form of regular vaccinations and by keeping a close eye on his well-being as you go along to prevent any potential problem from becoming serious. As already mentioned, you can give your dog a check-up while grooming him; checking his eyes, ears and skin can tell you a good deal about the state of his health. Make sure that your new puppy is healthy by taking him to see the vet as soon as possible; the vet will listen to his heart, look at his eyes and ears and check his faeces for any evidence of abnormalities such as parasites.

Vaccinations

It is of the utmost importance that your puppy is started on a programme of vaccination. They are very vulnerable to disease and should not be allowed to go outside or have any contact with unvaccinated dogs before they have had the full course as recommended by your vet. Vaccination is done three to four times between the ages of 12 and 14 weeks and guards against many life-threatening diseases.

Rabies – This is a deadly virus which attacks the nervous system and can affect all mammals. In many places, such as the U.K. and parts of Europe, the disease has been virtually eradicated, so vaccination will only be given where the disease is endemic.

The puppy should be vaccinated at 3 months with a booster around 10 months, followed by a further booster at approximately 1–3 years.

Canine Distemper – Often fatal, this is a viral disease which causes problems to the respiration, intestines and the nervous system. It is vital that your puppy is vaccinated every 3 weeks until he is 12–14 weeks old, followed by an annual booster. This is a multi-vaccine which protects from **Canine Hepatitis**, a virus which attacks the liver, and **Parainfluenza** which is the broad term for a group of viral and bacterial diseases which cause kennel cough, and which is similar to our common cold. **Canine Parvovirus** is a dangerous disease which attacks the intestines and can be fatal to puppies. Some vets vaccinate for Parvo separately at up to 5 months. **Leptospirosis** is a bacterial disease which can cause kidney and liver failure. Some vets don't vaccinate for this until 9 weeks.

There are other vaccines which your vet may advise, but this is largely dependent on where you live. Examples are **Lyme Disease**, which is carried by ticks and transmitted through

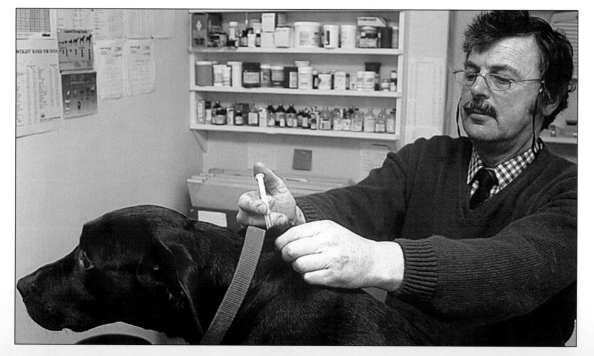

Signs of Illness

The more you get to know your dog the easier it is to sense when he is unwell. He may not be as lively as usual or he may hide himself away when he is usually under your feet. Watch closely, and you will notice if he presents any of the following symptoms:-

Excessive vomiting
Loss of appetite
Pain in the mouth
Weight loss, both sudden or prolonged, weight gain
Fever/lassitude, laboured breathing
Pain
Prolonged diarrhoea
Coughing

Choking
Sneezing
Frothing at the mouth
Increased urination/inability to urinate
Itching, scratching and head-shaking
Lameness
Fits
Eye discharge

Obesity

If you follow the preceding advice on feeding, your dog should not become fat. A healthy, balanced diet, tailored to suit his breed, physique and lifestyle, coupled with daily exercise, will help him to maintain his natural weight. It is most important to his well-being that he is not allowed to gain weight as obesity, as in human beings, can trigger or worsen other health problems such as heart disease, arthritis and diabetes, as well as certain skin disorders. It also reduces the dog's quality of life, making him miserable and listless.

To test if your dog is overweight, run your fingers along his ribcage; if you can't feel them he is overweight. Likewise, if you stand over him and he is lacking a pronounced waistline, he is overweight.

If your dog is slightly overweight, cut down his food consumption. Either reduce his total intake by at least 40 per cent (in which case it is a good idea to split the meals up into two or three small ones to fool him that he isn't hungry), or you can mash up some fresh

Opposite above: Good feeding, exercise, preventive medicine and vigilance will keep your dog free from illness and ensure a long happy life. This Irish Setter is a picture of health with his bright eyes and shiny coat.

Below: You should never delay starting your puppy on a course of vaccinations against fatal diseases. This Labrador Retriever is having his yearly booster.

Right: The same dog is now having his heart and lungs checked.

Below right: After cutting her paw, this little dog is having her temperature taken to check that no infection is present.

a bite and can affect much of the body, and **Coronavirus**, another intestinal disease which can prove fatal to puppies.

Signs of Life

There are times when your dog may appear a little off-colour, which could be indicative of something more serious. By learning to read his vital signs you could very well save his life.

Heartbeat – A dog's normal heartbeat is in the range of between 80 and 140 beats per minute. To feel for the beat, place you hand around the chest under the elbow. Set a stop watch to one minute, and count the beats. Anything significantly higher than 140 should be considered serious

and you should consult your vet immediately.

Respiration – Watch the dog's chest and listen to his breathing. If the chest is rising and falling at a dramatic rate, or the breathing appears laboured, take him to the vet at once.

Temperature – Put a little lubricating jelly on the end of a thermometer and insert it into the rectum at a depth of no more than 2 inches (5cm). Keeping the dog still, hold it there for two minutes. The normal temperature should be between 100.5 and 102°F (38–39°C); if it reads anything over 103°F (39.5°C), treat as serious and take the dog to the vet immediately.

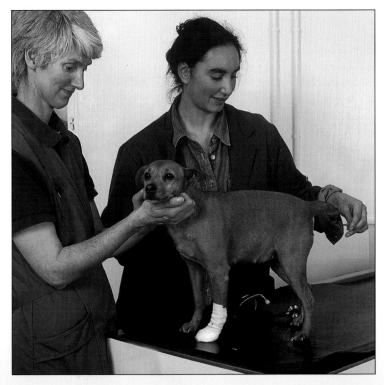

Far left: As in human beings, obesity in dogs is a health risk leading to heart disease and joint problems which will result in the dog leading a miserable and inactive life. This little Corgi is very overweight and needs to be put on a special diet specially designed for him with the help of the vet.

Left: Take your dog for a yearly professional check-up. The best time is when he is due for his booster vaccinations.

Below: It is most important to control fleas; not only do they make the host animal itchy and uncomfortable, they can also cause severe skin allergies as well as spreading tapeworms. This is because the tapeworm larvae live inside the flea which in turn is ingested by the dog.

Opposite: Some flea controls now work internally and can be administered by injection or a tablet, though most wormers come in tablet form. Some dogs don't mind taking medicine, in which case the jaws should be gently parted and the tablet placed on the back of the tongue when the dog will swallow it. Alternatively, it may be better to grind the tablet up and mix it with a small amount of a favourite food.

vegetables and use them to bulk up the rest of the food, or use one of the proprietory low-calorie foods which are high in fibre. Gradually increase his exercise (this is a vital part of weight loss), and over several days take him for short workouts, beginning with 5 minutes, building up to 10, and finally to 30 minutes, making the exercise more strenuous as the dog becomes fitter. Once he has reached 30 minutes, keep this up every day as a brisk walk or play in the park, monitoring his progress and stopping when he shows signs of tiring. If you keep to this routine you will be surprised at how quickly he loses weight and you will notice his new-found energy and athleticism. If he is very overweight, consult your vet who will put him on a special diet and advise regular check-ups and weigh-ins. To weigh your dog, crouch down and gather him up, supporting his rear and chest. Stand with him on the scales and deduct your own weight from the total to find out what his weight is.

Skin Problems

Fleas – When giving your dog his regular check-up while grooming, it is important that you look at his skin. A sure sign that something is amiss is

excessive itching and scratching. Then the obvious thing to look for is flea infestation and you can confirm this by running a fine-toothed comb over the dog's coat when you may catch some of the offenders. Concentrate on the rump and the area between the back legs and around the neck where you may also find evidence in the form of a reddish-black substance which consists of blood and flea faeces. The flea is

a very common parasite and plagues many animals besides cats and dogs. They survive by sucking the animal's blood and the bite causes an itchy irritation. Sometimes the dog may develop an allergy to the flea's saliva which will make him scratch frantically, resulting in sore and weeping skin. The flea, if eaten by the dog, is also responsible for the spread of tapeworms, so if your dog has fleas you should worm him as well.

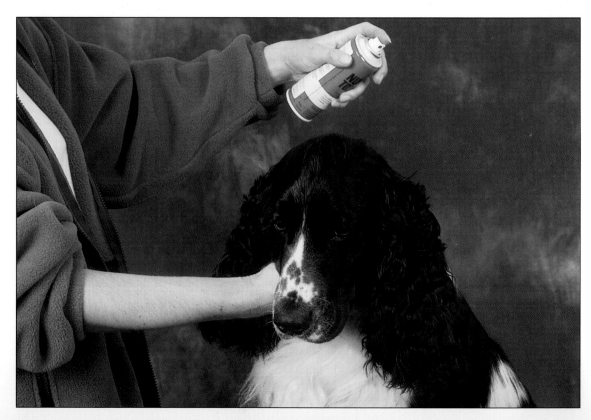

Common Parasites

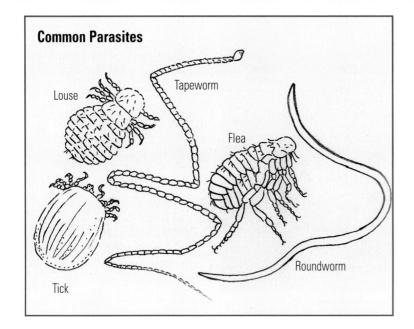

Louse

Tapeworm

Flea

Roundworm

Tick

spray. Then, with a pair of tweezers, grasp the tick just above the mouth parts, pulling it out sharply and making sure that you have removed the mouth parts as well.

Mites – These are tiny parasites which can only be detected under a microscope. There are two varieties, *demodex* and *sarcoptes* and both types cause mange. They occur naturally in all dogs, living in the hair follicles and under the skin and only become a problem then the dog's immunity is at a low ebb due to illness or even an incorrect diet. The mites multiply rapidly,

causing itching and hair loss and can lead to serious skin infections. They may also transfer to human beings. During grooming you may notice your dog has some bald patches which are sore and crusty, and he may be scratching frantically. Pay a visit to the vet who will take a skin scrape to examine under a microscope when all should be revealed. Mites can be treated with pesticide shampoos and other treatments can be injected or given orally.

Lice – These are particular varieties of lice which only affect the dogs in your home; they

The flea is quite a difficult pest to eradicate as it spends a part of its life cycle living apart from the dog, laying its eggs deep in the weave of your carpet. Merely to treat the dog is not enough. Start by thoroughly vacuuming the carpet, paying particular attention to the edges where fleas tend to congregate. Wash the dog's bedding and treat the carpet with a household flea-killer (your vet will recommend one which is safe for pets), applying it over the carpet and especially around the edges. Dispose of the vacuum cleaner bag when you have finished, preferably by burning it.

Next treat the dog. There is a huge variety of preparations on the market, but it is advisable to consult your vet. There is one type which can be sprayed onto the dog which is very effective and lasts for months and there is an anti-flea drug which can be administered to your pet by either tablet or injection. These are becoming very popular, are effective for up to a year and dispense with the need for sprays and powders.

Shampooing your dog regularly, though no more than once a month, will also help keep the flea population down. You may wish to buy a special flea shampoo, but others are just as effective. When he is dry,

comb him through thoroughly to catch any fleas which may have survived. Combing is also a good way of keeping fleas at bay as the combing action breaks the fleas' delicate legs, when they drop off and die.

Ticks – Are most common in the countryside where they inhabit woods and long grasses, fields and hedgerows, attaching themselves to dogs as they run by. The tick causes a great deal of irritation and can be particularly harmful as in some areas it is a carrier of Lyme Disease. If this is prevalent where you live, ask your vet to vaccinate your dog against it.

Ticks are easy to spot; they attach themselves to the hair and sink their mouths into the dog's skin to suck his blood. Its stomach becomes engorged with blood until it resembles a large apple pip. It will eventually drop off and attach itself to another animal, but it is desirable to kill it before this stage is reached.

If your dog frequents areas where ticks are prevalent, check him over, paying particular attention to the underside and legs. Once detected, dab the tick with alchohol, vodka, methylated spirits or apply a flea spray which kills ticks as well, leaving for a few minutes or as recommended if you are using a

cannot live on cats or humans. There are two kinds, one which bites the skin, feeding on the skin flakes, and the sucking louse which will cause even more irritation to the dog. Lice are relatively large, approximately 0.08in (2mm) long, and they lay eggs or nits which stick to the base of the dog's hair until they hatch. Treatment is with insecticide sprays or baths as recommended by your vet.

Gastric and Intestinal Disorders

Worms – These types of worm are parasitic, living in the dog's intestines. They are extremely common, puppies are even born with them or pick them up early from their mother's milk. Unless the adult worms are present in the dog's faeces, there is little other evidence that he has this problem; the only way is for your vet to examine the faeces under a microscope. To keep a dog free from these pests, a regular worming programme is vital. Your vet will recommend the correct wormers to use as well as the correct dosage. From the age of 4 weeks, treat your puppy for roundworms and repeat the treatment until he is 6 months old. Pregnant bitches will require a special worming programme and all adult dogs should be wormed every 6 months. Most wormers supplied by the vet will get rid of the most common varieties your dog is likely to pick up, the most usual being roundworms and tapeworms.

Roundworms – Several of these parasites inhabit the dog's small intestine, the most important belonging to the *ascarid* family; but some varieties, such as *toxacara*, also infest the large intestine, while others live in the blood vessels and respiratory tract. They feed on digested food passing through the dog's intestine and are most harmful to puppies, the worms being

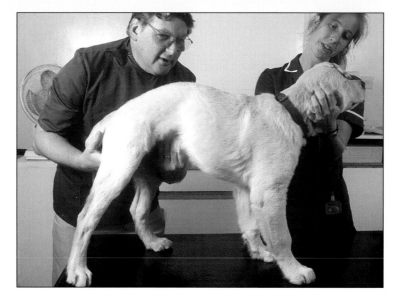

capable of passing through the gut wall, through the blood supply to the liver and lungs where they are coughed up and swallowed, repeating the process. Puppies may develop liver infections such as hepatitis, pneumonia and fits and obstruction of the intestine may also occur. In adults, the worms migrate to the muscles where they lie dormant as cysts and in pregnant bitches the worms attack the embryo and settle in the puppy's lungs, which is the reason why virtually all puppies are born with them present.

This type of worm is harmful to children as they may become encysted in the child's eye, in severe cases causing eye loss. However, this is thankfully rare, and can be avoided by immediately disposing of your dog's faeces, washing your hands thoroughly before handling food, and ensuring that your children wash their hands regularly. They should be trained not to put their hands in their mouths after touching the dog.

Hookworms and Whipworms

Both live in the intestine and are invisible to the naked eye so can only be detected by faecal examination. Both can cause diarrhoea and the hookworm can cause anaemia, both being the result of poor hygiene. They should be treated by your vet.

Left: Dogs will eat virtually anything and for this reason are prone to intestinal blockages. The vet is feeling for lumps which may indicate that this is the case.

Below: Excessive vomiting or diarrhea can lead to dehydration. A dog may need to be put on a drip for a while to replenish vital fluids.

Opposite: Conjunctivitis is a common disorder in dogs and can easily be cured with eye drops or ointment. Any sign of eye discomfort should be investigated by a vet as soon as possible.

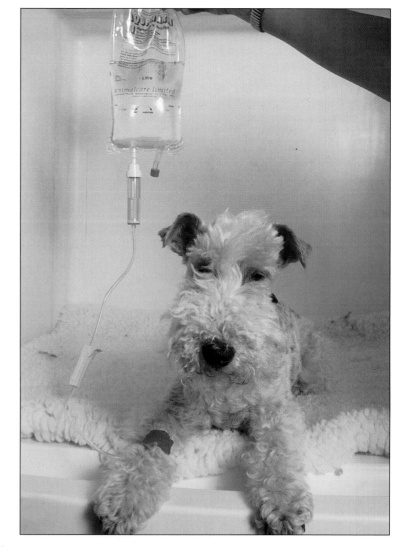

Heartworms – *Angiostrongylus* is a potentially fatal parasite. It lives in the blood vessels and is transmitted by slugs which have been eaten. The larvae leave the dog via the lungs when they are coughed up and swallowed, eventually ending up in the faeces. These are difficult to treat as the worms live in the dog's circulatory system and a drug administered to kill the worms in the dog's bloodstream could well cause a thrombosis. It is therefore necessary for the vet to treat him in his surgery where he can be monitored carefully.

Tapeworms – *Dipylidium caninum* is picked up when a dog inadvertently eats fleas in which the tapeworm larvae have developed. The worm is composed of segments which resemble grains of rice. They can cause itching and discomfort around the anus and the segments are clearly visible in the faeces. It is advisable to treat your dog for tapeworms regularly, and eradicating fleas will greatly help the process.

Bloat – This is a serious condition and should be treated as an emergency. At the first sign, take your dog to the vet immediately. Gastric dilatation and volvulus (GDV) occurs when the stomach becomes bloated with air, causing it to rotate and in effect blocking the escape of air from the stomach. Signs to look out for are a heavily distended stomach, and the dog retching without producing vomit. He will be in severe discomfort and the condition can lead to shock and even death. Surgery is required to decompress the stomach and to ensure that it is returned to its correct position. Bloat is most common in the larger, deep-chested breeds.

Vomiting – All dogs vomit from time to time and they habitually eat such extraordinary things that it is just as well that they do. They also tend to vomit when they have overeaten. Eating grass to induce vomiting is often an indication that your dog is unwell, so keep a close eye on him. However, and to add to the confusion, they also eat grass because they like it.

If your dog has been vomiting, leave him to rest in a quiet place and don't give any food for 24 hours apart from a little water. Then reintroduce food again slowly, choosing

bland foods such as chicken and rice. Once fully recovered he can be returned to his normal diet.

If he cannot stop vomiting and continues to do so after fasting, or if there is blood present, take him to the vet immediately as the cause may be serious, indicating poisoning, an intestinal obstruction, kidney or liver failure, inflammation of the pancreas or an infectious disease such as parvovirus. If the dog has been sick for a prolonged period he will be very dehydrated and your vet may decide to put him on a drip.

Diarrhoea – All dogs suffer from diarrhoea at some time or another, the usual cause being overeating or a change of diet. In these cases, follow the same procedure as if he had been vomiting. If diarrhoea persists over the next two days, he may be suffering from something more serious such as worms, kidney disease, cancer or a viral disease, so consult your vet.

Flatulence – This is usually caused by overeating or a reaction to diet. A little wind is perfectly natural, but if flatulence becomes a problem, feed small meals more often and avoid soy-based products which are a prime cause of the trouble.

Anal sacs – These are glands situated on either side of the anus and contain an unpleasant-smelling discharge, which is normally expelled when the dog defecates. In some cases, however, the sacs become blocked causing discomfort. The dog will begin to drag his bottom along the floor or continually lick his anus. When this occurs, take him to the vet who will empty the sacs which is a simple procedure; ask him to show you how to do this as the problem is likely to recur. Never ignore this as the sacs may become infected; if they do, antibiotics will be required.

Urinary Disorders

Keep a watchful eye on your dog's urinary habits; any changes such as straining to go, more frequent than normal urination, or signs of blood in the urine should be regarded as serious and may require immediate

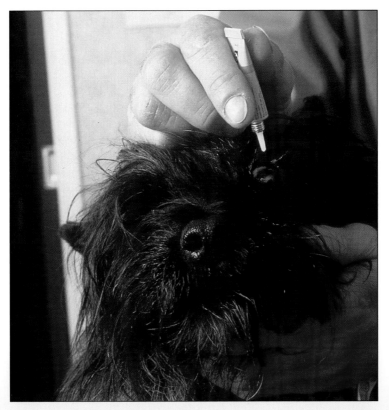

veterinary attention or even surgery. An infection of the urinary tract could be the cause of any of these symptoms as well as disease of the prostate gland in male dogs and a blockage caused by kidney stones can be fatal if not treated at once. Other diseases which cause increased urination are kidney failure and diabetes, both common in older dogs. An indication of the presence of these is increased thirst. While diabetes can be kept in check with insulin injections, kidney failure will eventually cause death, but with a low protein diet, plenty of fluids and regular exercise the progress of the disease can be slowed down.

Incontinence can easily be distinguished from a behavioural problem because the dog will leak in his sleep, leaving wet patches. However, there are many causes of incontinence such as prostate trouble in males and cystitis predominately in females, the latter being curable with medication. Older dogs may become incontinent due to a variety of causes, many listed above; all can be controlled to a certain extent and you can help the problem by taking your dog for plenty of walks, or by letting him out as often as possible to relieve himself.

The Eye

The dog's eye is very similar in structure to our own, so it follows that similar problems will occur. Keep a close check on your dog's eyes, checking for discharge, redness, swelling or cloudiness. A healthy eye should be clear and bright, the white parts should be white not pink and the under parts of the eyelids should be a healthy pink with no redness or inflammation. If your dog does lose his sight for whatever reason, it is not the end of the world; all the dog's senses are sharp, particularly those of smell and hearing and blind dogs can manage quite well. They will soon memorize the layout of your house and will happily go for a walk while staying close to your side.

Conjunctivitis – This is one of the most common diseases of the eye in both humans and dogs. It is an inflammation of the conjunctiva, the membrane lining the eyelids. The infection can be caused by a foreign body in the eye, or a scratch or tumour on the eyelid: it can also occur because of a congenital disorder which is a deformity of the eyelid, *entropion*, in which the eyelid grows inwards, causing the eyelashes to scrape the surface of the eye or *ectropion* where the eyelid turns outward. Tears then flood in a pouch formed by the lid, leaving the cornea unlubricated so that it dries out. Both can be corrected by surgery. In other cases the eyelashes may grow in the wrong direction, called *trichiasis*, causing pain and redness. The hairs are removed using electrolysis, relieving the suffering. Conjunctivitis can be treated with eyedrops or ointment prescribed by your vet.

Dry Eye – Keratoconjunctivitis is a condition when the eyes don't produce enough tears to adequately lubricate the eye. Symptoms are redness, severe discomfort and a greenish discharge. This should be treated at once to save the eye from permanent damage. Treatment with medication can be given to keep the eyes moist.

Glaucoma – This is caused by a disorder of the drainage system inside the eye. Some of the drainage outlets can become blocked, causing the fluid to build up to dangerous levels inside the eye, when it becomes painfully stretched. The dog will require immediate treatment in the form of either surgery or drugs to reduce the fluid to save his sight. Symptoms to look out for are swelling, excessive tear production, pain and sensitivity to light.

Cataracts – This is usually a condition of old age. However, it can be hereditary or caused by a mother's poor condition during pregnancy. Symptoms are a cloudy cast which appears over the lens which can be surgically treated in severe cases.

Disorders of the Retina – This is an important part of the eye, being the means by which dogs are able to see. The most common disease of the retina is progressive retinal atrophy (PRA) in which the blood supply to the light-sensitive cells gradually withers away causing the cells to die. There are two forms of the disease, central and generalized, and both will lead to reduced vision and may cause total blindness. Dogs affected in this way may also have cataracts. Unfortunately there is no known cure.

Corneal Injury – These are caused by external forces such as a scratch to the eye from an overhanging branch. Damage to the cornea should be treated immediately as the eye may become infected and ulcerated leading to blindness. Prompt action will save a dog's sight.

Dental Care

Clean your dog's teeth every time you groom him. Use a small toothbrush or flannel cloth and a

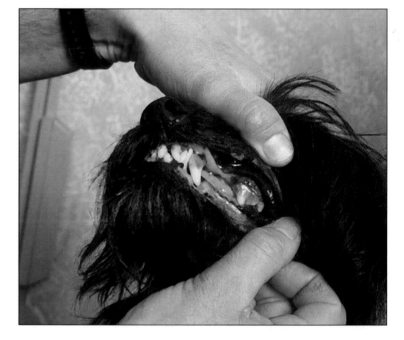

toothpaste for dogs and check that the teeth are clean with no tartar build-up. This irritates the gums resulting in a disease called gingivitis which can also be caused by the milk teeth not falling out when they should. Get your vet to check your dog's teeth every year.

To keep the teeth clean and the gums healthy, let your dog chew on a knuckle bone or hide chew which will also exercise the jaw. Your dog is likely to have bad breath if there are problems with his teeth; other signs are drooling, pain when eating, nasal discharge or a swollen jaw. If he has any of these, take him to the vet.

Left: Clean your dog's teeth regularly to avoid a build-up of tartar, the main cause of gum disease.

Below: This dog's teeth have a build-up of tartar which will need to be removed by the vet.

Opposite
Left: Dogs are not exempt from ear problems. Check them regularly and keep the outer areas clean.

Right: Like us, dogs suffer from disorders of the joints such as arthritis, which can be alleviated by a change of diet and anti-inflammatory drugs.

Disorders of the Ears

Deafness – The main cause of deafness in dogs is hereditary, through selective breeding, and is particularly common in dogs which are predominately white such as Dalmations. It is so common that you should always have a dog's hearing tested before buying it. Infection of the inner ear can also cause deafness, nerve damage and loss of balance.

The ear consists of four different parts: the flap, the external ear canal, middle and inner ear. The ear flap is vulnerable to injury and can easily be torn on branches when dogs run through undergrowth;

Facts About Neutering

Neutering is permanent sterilization; it involves the removal of the testicles in males and the removal of the uterus and ovaries in females. It is now a very safe operation and causes little discomfort.

There are many myths surrounding the process; here are some answers to common concerns.

Obesity
Neutering need not cause obesity. Neutered dogs may use less calories, so reduce their food and give them plenty of exercise to keep them fit.

Depression
Neutering does not cause depression; in fact a dog will usually be happier and more interested in play rather than constantly occupied with the desire to mate.

Reduction of territorial instincts
Once again, there is no evidence to support this. The dog is likely to be even more vigilant, as his thoughts won't be occupied with mating.

Benefits
Neutering dogs will benefit both males and females far more than leaving them entire. It virtually eradicates the chances of prostate and testicular cancers and behavioural problems such as roaming, mounting other dogs and fighting. Females are unlikely to develop breast or uterine cancer, and blood staining will no longer be a problem in your home, neither will unwanted gentlemen callers or the risk of pregnancy.

Both males and females are less likely to stray, thereby reducing the risk of road and other accidents.

Castration on the other hand will not make a dog less boisterous; this can only be achieved through training.

Veterinarians have kept the cost of neutering down to a minimum to encourage people to have their pets neutered; if you cannot afford this, there are organizations which offer very low-cost neutering.

Many thousands of unwanted dogs are destroyed each year due to unplanned pregnancy. Reduce these numbers by having your dog neutered!

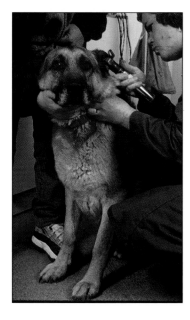

in case of injury, hold a towel tightly over the wound and take to the vet immediately for stitching. Haematomas are another problem connected with the ear flaps; these are lumps caused by a small injury or by excessive head-shaking which fill with blood, and are common in older dogs. Haematomas do not disappear of their own accord, but must be treated by your vet as delay may cause the ear to become deformed.

Otitis Externa – This is an inflammation of the external ear canal caused by ear mites, yeast and bacterial infections, and is also common in dogs who like to swim. In this instance, it can be avoided by drying inside the ears thoroughly, the best method being a mixture of half vinegar half rubbing alcohol which, when inserted, helps to dry out the ear. Signs of otitis externa start with head-shaking and scratching the offending ear which may be inflamed and painful to touch, emitting a foul-smelling discharge. The ear mite produces a thick discharge which has a gritty consistency. At the first sign of this disease, take you dog to the vet.

Cleaning the Ears
Only clean your dog's ears if they are dirty or if there is a waxy discharge. Don't insert anything into the ear canal, use a piece of damp cotton wool to clean around the outer area of the external ear canal.

Disorders of the Bones
Osteoarthritis – The most common bone disease, this manifests itself in inflammation of the joints. It is a degenerative disease most common in older dogs, the underlying causes being an old injury, an inherited malformation, such as hip dysplasia, or simple wear and tear. Symptoms are an initial stiffness after rest which eventually wears off after

Right: The German Shepherd is a breed which suffers from hereditary disorders, in particular hip dysplasia. Reputable breeders are attempting to eradicate these defects by only breeding from dogs which are free of them.

exercise. In more extreme cases the dog will walk with a stilted gait or have a pronounced limp. A visit to your vet will determine the severity of your dog's condition when he will usually be given anti-inflammatory drugs, a diet sheet and a specially designed exercise regime.

Hip Dysplasia – This is an inherited abnormality which mostly affects the larger breeds, the most common example being the German Shepherd, who has been bred with a sloping rump. This abnormal positioning of the hip joint can be painful, particularly when arthritis inevitably sets in. In extreme cases surgery is required to re-build the joint; for less severe cases, the same treatment as for arthritis is usually given.

Back Pain – Like us, dogs also suffer from back pain. In some cases it may only be sore muscles resulting from strenuous activity, in others the dog may have a partially slipped disk when he may be reluctant to climb stairs or jump; he may also cry out when picked up. Complete rest and treatment with muscle relaxants and anti-inflammatory drugs will possibly be all that is required. However, if the disk has slipped severely the dog may suffer a partial or total paralysis, in which case urgent surgery is required.

Back pain is a common complaint in long-backed, short-legged breeds such as Corgis and Dachshunds.

Taking care of old dogs

The dog, if well cared for all his life, can live for anything up to 18 years. Like people, however, older dogs are likely to suffer from health problems, including kidney failure, diabetes, arthritis, cataracts as well and blindness and deafness. Most of these can be controlled with appropriate care and attention. Keep a close eye on your dog's health; if there are any abnormal changes, take him to the vet. If caught early, many diseases can be controlled. Give him regular gentle exercise; an old dog enjoys a walk as much as a young one. Feed him a healthy diet and watch his weight; fat dogs are much more likely to suffer from heart disease, kidney failure and diabetes. Old dogs don't need as many calories as they become less energetic, and there are proprietory foods especially designed for them.

Chapter Nine
First Aid

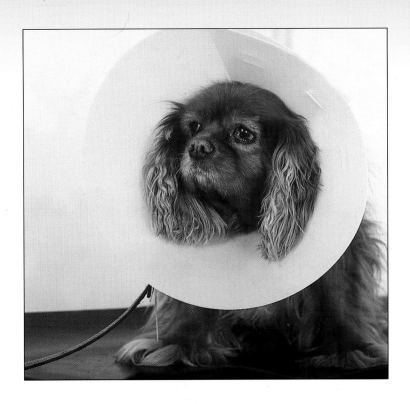

Dogs are by nature inquisitive and impetuous creatures who, being unable to reason for themselves, blunder foolishly into dangerous situations. To avoid disastrous consequences you will have to think for him. Where there is danger, put him on a leash. He will have little chance of survival if struck by a car and will at best sustain traumatic injuries in the form of fractures, cuts and bruises, excessive bleeding and internal damage.

Fighting dogs, particularly males, can inflict very serious injuries on one another; avoid this by keeping dogs leashed when fighting is likely to occur.

Many dogs sustain serious injuries in the home; keep them out of the kitchen when you are cooking. A large dog is quite capable of reaching the stove top when he could pull cooking pots over himself or touch hotplates, both equally disastrous. A small dog running around under your feet is also a hazard, causing you to trip and spill the contents of hot saucepans over him.

Don't leave dangerous or valuable objects lying where dogs can reach them; puppies in particular love to chew things up, and a small object may well

Above: By nature, dogs love chasing after sticks. However, don't allow them to chew them as this could result in splinters of wood being caught in the mouth. Worse still, a stick caught on the move could actually pierce the mouth and cause death. Many of these injuries are reported each year.

Top: If your dog is unfortunate enough to require suturing he may have to wear an Elizabethan collar until healing is complete. Its high sides will prevent him from pecking at the stitches, thus reducing the risk of infection.

stick in the windpipe causing choking or an intestinal blockage if swallowed. Keep appliances unplugged when not in use; any animal may receive a fatal shock if it starts chewing electric cables.

Keep all poisons and drugs locked safely away. If your dog does consume a poisonous substance, take him along to the vet immediately and bring the bottle or packaging with you. This will give the vet an indication of the correct treatment to give.

Heatstroke – In hot weather, dogs can rapidly overheat. Keep strenuous exercise to a minimum on hot days, and out of full sun. Never leave your dog in the motor-car even with the windows open as they are potential deathtraps. Even moderate temperatures in summer make the car a veritable oven and can cause brain damage and an agonizing death. If your dog has heatstroke don't dowse him in cold water; the shock could kill him. Lower the body temperature slowly and gradually using cool water, and place ice packs to the head and the back of the neck. Seek immediate veterinary assistance.

Fractures – If your dog is in severe pain and is loath to put weight on a leg he may have broken it. It is most important to keep him as still and as quiet as possible; struggling may cause more pain and damage. If the dog is small, lift him up gently, supporting the body but letting the damaged leg dangle. In the case of a larger dog, you will have to improvise a stretcher – a flat board will do – gently easing him onto it. In both cases consult the vet immediately. Do not attempt to make a splint for the injured limb – you could do even more damage. If you suspect a spinal injury, call the vet out to you.

Shock – Your dog could go into shock for a variety of reasons, including poisoning, heatstroke or an accident.

The dog will appear weak and cold to the touch and his gums may be a pale greyish colour. Keep him warm by loosely wrapping him in a blanket and take him to the vet immediately.

Drowning – Most dogs love to swim. However, they may occasionally get into trouble. If the dog appears lifeless in the water, pull him onto the bank and remove any discharge or blockages from the airway, pulling the tongue forward to drain the water from the lungs. If small, hold him upside down swinging him gently from side to side. Should he stop breathing, proceed with cardio-pulmonary resuscitation (CPR). (See page 72.)

Minor Wounds – Clip the hair surrounding the wound, cleaning it thoroughly and treat with antiseptic. Consult the vet if you are at all worried.

Deep Wounds – If your dog has a serious cut which is exposing

Above: Most dogs have dense coats and can quickly overheat. Never leave your dog in the car under any circumstances, not even with a window open, and don't leave him tied up in full sunlight. Prevent him from overexerting himself on hot days.

Right: Most dogs love swimming, particularly on a hot day, and most are excellent swimmers and rarely get into trouble. However, don't let them swim in rough seas or very cold water. If you are going boating it is a good idea to fit a harness or lifejacket.

underlying tissue and bleeding profusely and if the area can be bandaged, cover it with a thick pad of clean gauze, wrapping a bandage tightly around it to stem the blood flow. If the wound cannot be bandaged, hold the gauze over the wound and apply pressure. **Do not apply a tourniquet, you could do even more damage.** Rush the dog to the vet.

Burns – May be caused by fire, or a spillage of boiling water or oil. Cool the burns with cold water, then apply a cold compress while calling the vet.

Seizures – This is abnormal activity in the brain caused by epilepsy, brain tumour, or a head injury. The symptoms include frothing at the mouth, twitching, whimpering, vomiting and uncontrolled urination and defecation. Don't be tempted to touch the dog; he is not in control of his actions and could well swallow his tongue. Stand back until the seizure has subsided – they don't usually last long. Afterwards, take the dog to the vet to investigate the cause of the problem.

Poisoning – As mentioned before, a dog will eat almost anything, so poisoning is quite a common occurrence. Symptoms are vomiting, diarrhoea, foaming at the mouth, laboured breathing, muscular twitching, weakness and maybe fits. Take the dog to the vet immediately and bring the poison in its container with you if you know what it is.

Electric Shock – Commonly caused by chewing through an electric cable, the dog may collapse, lose consciousness and stop breathing due to heart failure, or he may go into shock having suffered burns to the mouth. Turn off, and unplug the appliance before

going anywhere near him. If he has stopped breathing administer CPR (page 72) and call the vet immediately.

Choking – A small object caught in the airway will cause the dog to choke. Symptoms may be violent head-shaking, foaming at the mouth, gagging and retching. He may attempt to remove the object with his paw. His gums may turn blue or grey from lack of oxygen and he may collapse. If you can see the offending object, remove it quickly, taking care that he doesn't bite you. If the dog isn't too heavy, hold him upside down and shake him. If he is too large, give him a sharp tap on the back of the neck between the shoulders which may dislodge the object. If this fails, rush him to the vet.

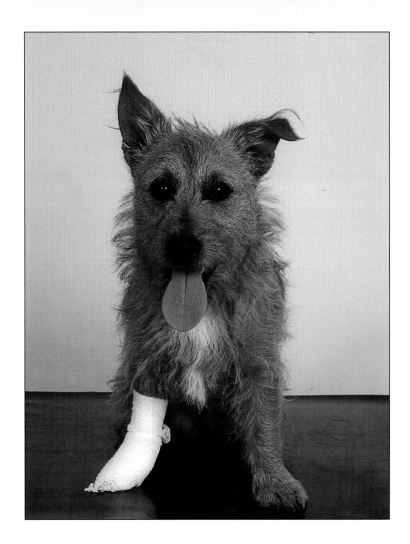

Right: If your dog has sustained a deep cut, put a gauze pad over the wound, then bind it tightly with a bandage and take him to the vet for sutures.

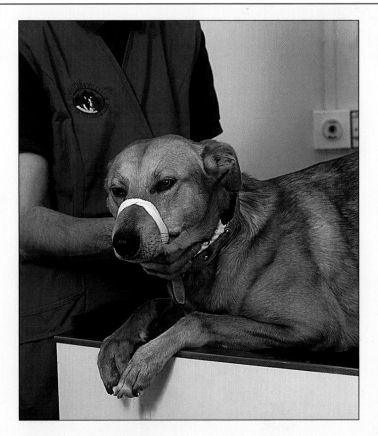

Applying a Muzzle

Before administering any kind of first aid you should apply a muzzle, as animals in pain are unpredictable and may bite. Keeping your face well away from the dog in case he snaps, apply a muzzle. If you don't have a ready-made one, take a length of rope or bandage and tie it once around the dog's nose and mouth with the knot at the top; then wrap it around again and tie underneath. Secure the ends behind the head. Check that the dog can breathe normally; if not, re-tie so that the muzzle is looser.

Unconsciousness and Loss of Heartbeat

Check first for the vital signs (page 61) to establish that the dog is alive. Place him on his side, clear his airway and bring his tongue forward. Establish if there are any broken bones and if so call the vet; if not, you may carefully pick him up and take him to the vet. If there are no signs of life (the dog is not breathing and has no heartbeat), administer **Cardio-Pulmonary Resuscitation (CPR)**. This is a combination of mouth-to-nose resuscitation and cardiac massage. First remove any mucus and obstruction from the airway, pulling the tongue forward. Place your mouth over the dog's nose and breathe steadily into it for 2–3 seconds, waiting another 2–3 seconds for air to be expelled from the lungs. If the dog fails to resume breathing and/or there is no heartbeat you will need to apply cardiac massage. Place your hands on the chest just behind the elbow and press down firmly five times with a 1-second interval. Next repeat the mouth-to-nose sequence, repeating it for 10 minutes or until the heart starts beating again. Once the heart has re-started, cease cardiac massage but carry on with the mouth-to-nose resuscitation until the dog is breathing normally. This could take up to an hour. While you are proceeding with this, ask another person to call the vet for you.

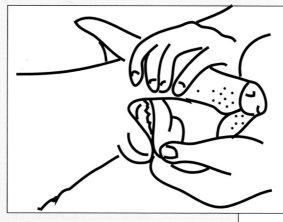

Mouth-to-Nose Resuscitation

Remove any obstructions from the dog's nose and breathe steadily into it for 2–3 seconds. Wait for 2–3 seconds for the air to be expelled from the lungs. Continue until the dog is breathing normally.

Clearing the airway

Bring the tongue forward so that the airway is clear.

Expelling water from a dog which isn't breathing

Remove objects from the nose and mouth, pulling the tongue forward. If small, swing dog back and forward by the hind legs until water is expelled. If necessary, use mouth-to-nose resuscitation and cardiac massage.

Cardiac Massage

If the dog fails to resume breathing, apply cardiac massage. Place one hand on top of the other and press down gently but firmly. Do this five or six times with 1-second intervals in between. Alternate with the mouth-to-nose resuscitation.

Chapter Ten
Breeding

Breeding from your own dog is not something to be recommended: there are many thousands of unwanted puppies born every year, all requiring good homes. If you are determined to breed, make yourself aware of the risks and facts surrounding the process. Breeding, particularly from pedigree animals, can be extremely complicated and you are advised to speak to an expert on the subject. There are books available which provide detailed information on canine reproduction, pregnancy and postnatal care.

Before you begin, make sure that you pre-arrange good homes for the resulting puppies, and be prepared to keep them if their new owners decide against taking them. They are your responsibility and you must not add to the problem of growing numbers of unwanted dogs in rehoming centres.

Above: Before mating your female, make sure that she and the male are free from hereditary diseases and parasites.

Right: These Dalmation puppies are adorable, but be aware that they can be born deaf due to an hereditary defect.

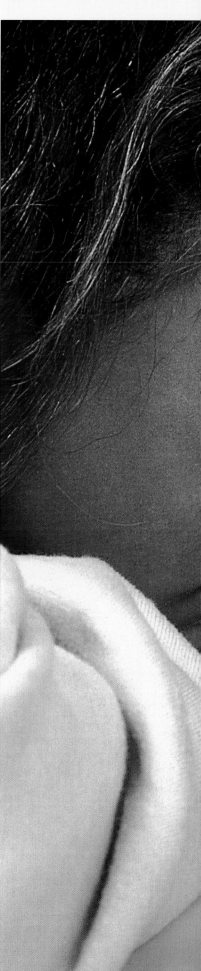

Well before putting the process of reproduction into action, read up on the hereditary disorders your particular breed may suffer from. If your female has any of these herself, don't breed from her, the disorder will be passed to the puppies and may be even more severe. Once it is established that your female is healthy you should look for a mate which is also free from these problems. Consult a reputable breeder who is aware of the pitfalls of breeding dogs with hereditary diseases. Watch the male closely and make sure that he has a good disposition. Don't mate your female with a dog that is aggressive or timid. He should be sociable and get on well with other dogs. Once you have chosen a suitable mate, have both dogs thoroughly vetted. This will involve x-rays, blood and eye tests as well as examination for evidence of brucellosis (a sexually-transmitted disease causing

sterility) and parasites, and that they are treated accordingly, all of which is a costly business. Make sure that both dogs are registered with the appropriate kennel club for your country as it is far more difficult to find homes for unregistered puppies. Don't be tempted to mate your female with any old dog just because it is free.

Even if your dog is not a pedigree breed you will be well advised to have both male and female checked over by a vet, making sure that both are free from parasites and that they are fully vaccinated against fatal diseases.

This is by no means an in-depth guide on the subject of breeding and should be treated as initial advice only. There are many books on the subject offering excellent advice and information. In addition, your vet should also be able to advise you on most of the important aspects of the subject.

Above: This Golden Retriever has six hungry puppies to feed and will require a special diet to help her produce sufficient milk for them as well as giving her the energy to cope with her mischievous new family.

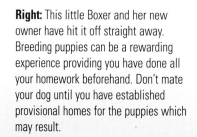

Right: This little Boxer and her new owner have hit it off straight away. Breeding puppies can be a rewarding experience providing you have done all your homework beforehand. Don't mate your dog until you have established provisional homes for the puppies which may result.